Praise for *Everything I Know About Success I Learned from Napoleon Hill*

"The testament to Don Green's generosity of spirit is shown through the millions of people whose lives have been positively impacted by him. From a brief encounter over a banker's desk to working with him side by side in promoting the timeless wisdom of Napoleon Hill, all who have the great fortune to meet and work with Don have found their own success as a result of his graciousness and guidance. Now he shares his brilliance and lifelong formula for Success with you in *Everything I Know About Success I Learned from Napoleon Hill*."

—Sharon Lechter,
coauthor of *Rich Dad, Poor Dad* series,
Three Feet from Gold, editor *Napoleon Hill's Outwitting the Devil*,
and Member Presidents Financial Literacy Board

"This book could literally transform your life."

—Linda Forsythe,
publisher, *Mentors Magazine*

"Mr. Green is a true wordsmith. Everyone should read this book."

—Bob Proctor,
author, motivational speaker, part of book, *The Secret*

"Great message—Great wisdom."

—Bill Bartmann,
author, speaker, billionaire businessman, at one time
on Forbes richest people in America

"Don has a simple way of sharing meaningful insights that make you want to stand up and cheer."

—Ron Glosser,
former bank CEO and CEO of Hershey Foundation

"This book is worth its weight in gold."

—Joe Dudley, Sr.,
founder of Dudley Products, one of the largest minority
owned cosmetic companies in the United States,
author, philanthropist, Horatio Alger Award Winner

"This book can be described in one word—Tremendous."

—Tracey Jones,
author, CEO of Tremendous Life Books

"This book is proof that dynamite comes in small packages."

—Les Brown,
noted author, motivational speaker

"An absolutely enjoyable read."

—Brian Tracy,
author of numerous bestselling books,
speaker, and consultant to major corporations

"This book has the potential to impact the lives of many; great job Don."

—John Assaraf,
New York Times bestselling author of *Having It All* and other books

"A great book filled with simple, time-tested principles."

—Leah O'Brien,
three-time Olympic Gold Medalist

"Don Green is a masterful storyteller."

—Gary Goldstein,
movie producer of such movies as *Pretty Woman*
starring Richard Gere, and other films

"A truly inspirational read."

—Frank Shankwitz,
founder of Make a Wish Foundation

"The perfect book at the perfect time."

—Ruben Gonzalez,
four-time Olympian

"W. Clement Stone personally hand-picked Don Green to direct my grandfather's Foundation. While I have been truly pleased with Don Green's directorship, I have always been curious as to why Mr. Stone chose him for the task—until now. *Everything I Know About Success I Learned from Napoleon Hill* shows that Don Green's life experience personified Napoleon Hill's philosophy, making him the ideal person to spread the science of personal achievement across the world. Mr. Stone chose wisely; no other person has worked as hard to preserve and promulgate the work of Napoleon Hill."

—Dr. J.B. Hill,
Napoleon Hill's grandson

"Life lessons come in two forms: theoretical lessons and life experiences. In *Everything I Know About Success I Learned from Napoleon Hill*, Don has married the theoretical and the practical into one powerful tool. He weaves the timeless truths from the master, Napoleon Hill, with his own life's experience of overwhelming success."

—Jim Stovall,
bestselling author, *The Ultimate Gift*

"What a great book! From the first few pages, one quickly realizes that true wealth is not found in one's bank account as much as it is discovered from a life well lived."

—Greg S. Reid,
coauthor *Three Feet from Gold* and *Napoleon Hill's Road to Riches*

"As president of the Napoleon Hill Foundation, it has been a pleasure to work with Don as executive director of the Napoleon Hill Foundation. For 12 years, Don has led the Foundation to an increased awareness of Dr. Hill's philosophy worldwide. Reading Don's book will be enjoyable and helpful to the reader."

—Jim Oleson,
retired stockbroker and financial advisor and
president of the Napoleon Hill Foundation

"Don Green's success stories stand out above all the rest. Nothing short of inspirational . . . from humble beginnings to the pinnacle of achievement. Don's use of the "Success System That Never Fails" has served him well. Read this book and reap the benefits from a lifetime of lessons learned. You will be the beneficiary of his legacy. Warning: Once you pick it up, you will not be able to put it down."

—Shane Morand,
Global Master Distributor, Organo Gold International

"Don Green has walked in the footsteps of, and sat in the chair of, Napoleon Hill and W. Clement Stone. That alone would not make him successful, were he not the consummate student, the tireless worker, and have the burning desire to succeed. Combine that with his wisdom and his ability to maintain the highest level of ethics. Don Green's career has been a book that has finally come to life. A book that will inspire you to a thousand new thoughts, and a million new dollars."

—Jeffrey Gitomer,
author of *The Little Red Book of Selling*

"In 1983 I became the first Executive Director of the re-established Napoleon Hill Foundation. I previously worked personally with Napoleon Hill for over 10 years, simultaneously working with W. Clement Stone for a total of 52 years. In the year 2000, it was time for me to retire from the Foundation. Having searched far and wide for a replacement who knew, understood, applied, and practiced successfully the Napoleon Hill Principles of Success, as well as sound business practices, The Board of Directors and I discovered it was to be one of our own. A person we could depend on, who could successfully carry on the dissemination and marketing of the Success Philosophy of Napoleon Hill, worldwide. His name . . . Don Green, a man who had served diligently, as one of our board members and now would change careers from being a successful bank president to dedicating all his efforts to Perpetuating the Philosophy of Success that Napoleon Hill formulated, and for the past 10 years he has done just that. A job well done, I and the Board of Directors are very proud of Don and his accomplishments and achievements for the Foundation."

—Michael J. Ritt, Jr.,
past executive director, Napoleon Hill Foundation

EVERYTHING
I KNOW ABOUT
SUCCESS
I LEARNED FROM
NAPOLEON
HILL

ESSENTIAL LESSONS FOR USING THE POWER OF POSITIVE THINKING

DON M. GREEN

Mc
Graw
Hill
Education

New York   Chicago   San Francisco   Lisbon   London
Madrid   Mexico City   Milan   New Delhi   San Juan
Seoul   Singapore   Sydney   Toronto

1 2 3 4 5 6 7 8 9 10   DOC/DOC   1 9 8 7 6 5 4 3

ISBN   978-0-07-181006-7
MHID   0-07-181006-4

e-ISBN   978-0-07-181007-4
e-MHID   0-07-181007-2

McGraw-Hill books are available at special quantity discounts to use as premiums
and sales promotions or for use in corporate training programs. To contact a repre-
sentative, please e-mail us at bulksales@mcgraw-hill.com.

This book is printed on acid-free paper.

To Phyl, my wife and best friend, who has
always been my inspiration.
To my daughter, Donna, who has made me a proud
parent and given joy to all who know her.
To my parents, brothers, and sister who helped provide
the experiences I have lived and enjoyed.

CONTENTS

FOREWORD

DON GREEN IS a gift to all who know him. And now you have an opportunity to receive that gift by reading *Everything I Know About Success I Learned from Napoleon Hill*. Don shares his personal story, proving that even with the most modest upbringing . . . you can achieve a lifetime of great achievement.

Don reveals the secrets and proven techniques for true success, drawing from the anecdotes and mini-biographies of many of the successful people who greatly influenced his life, like Napoleon Hill, W. Clement Stone, and Stephen R. Covey. He shares gems from these great teachers and adds his own real-life experiences in a down-to-earth approach that will speed you on your way to achieving your own greatest success. His stories will help you relive a time when neighbors helped neighbors in need and communities banned together during good times and bad . . . never asking for federal government assistance.

Don Green grew up in the rugged Appalachian Mountains, the son of an underground coal miner. While his parents had little formal education, they taught by example, infusing Don with their love, warmth, and instilled self-discipline, as well as their dedication to hard work and honesty, . . . creating the very best learning environment for their young son.

Don shares how his parents taught him that hard work never killed anyone, a message he heard many times as he grew up. Even though Don's parents never earned much money (very little actually), his mom had her house and car paid for and a fairly nice nest egg when she recently passed away. She proudly maintained her financial independence, paid her own bills, donated to charity on a regular basis, and reviewed all her financial statements and documents until just before her passing.

It is this spirit of self-determination and philanthropy that has guided Don throughout his life. He is the embodiment of and a living example of a true gentleman and an incredible teacher and mentor. His southern drawl adds color and life to his talent as a natural story-teller and draws you in so you can experience his world of dedication, contribution, and great success.

You will laugh as he shares the story of his pet bear escaping during his childhood entrepreneurial efforts in operating a zoo and souvenir stand. You will then see how those early entrepreneurial efforts blossomed into a lifetime of success and impressive accomplishment within the financial services industry as he became the president and CEO of a bank at the young age of 41. Today, as CEO of the Napoleon Hill Foundation, Don works tirelessly to promote the teachings of Napoleon Hill around the world, inspiring and instructing a new generation of entrepreneurs and achievers.

I am honored to have had the opportunity to work with and to learn from Don Green. His contribution to the world, for which he never seeks recognition, is a testament to success and his lifelong dedication to helping others. Read *Everything I Know About Success*

I Learned from Napoleon Hill and while you get to know this incredible man you will find yourself charting your own path to success.

—Sharon Lechter
Founder and CEO of Pay Your Family First
Author of *Save Wisely, Spend Happily*
Coauthor of *Rich Dad, Poor Dad* and 14 other books in the
Rich Dad series

And in cooperation with the Napoleon Hill Foundation:
Annotator of *Outwitting the Devil*,
and coauthor of *Three Feet from Gold*
Sharon@sharonlechter.com

ACKNOWLEDGMENTS

THIS BOOK IS the result of the many requests I have had over the years to share my experiences—that will hopefully help the readers duplicate and greatly exceed any success that I have been blessed to accomplish. At the same time it is important to learn from the mistakes of others, in this case my own which I learned to accept, not as failures but as lessons learned.

There are so many people who made contributions to this book that no matter how lengthy the list, I know I will miss many.

First the two students from UVA-Wise, Tosha Sturgill Wyatt and Brooke Lawson, for their technical skills used to put the words on the computer. Countless revisions dictated many copies and both of their work as part-time employees has contributed greatly to any success that may be accomplished with this book.

To Annedia Sturgill, who has always been there to see that the work is done on schedule and with the attitude that making a difference is what we do.

The Board of Trustees of the Napoleon Hill Foundation, Dr. Charles Johnson, James E. Oleson, Phil Fuentes, Mike Battle, and Attorney Robert W. Johnson, Jr. for their support and confidence in the mission of the Napoleon Hill Foundation.

The many individuals at McGraw-Hill who were professional and patient such as Donya Dickerson, Executive Editor; Ann Pryor, Senior Publicity Manager; and Daina Penikas, Senior Editing Supervisor. I owe a debt of gratitude.

Others who have helped and encouraged me along the way include: Chris Achua, Bill Bailles, Amy Bond, Debbie Collins, Judy Combs, Tim and Angel Cox, Diane Cornett, Amy Clark, Kim Deel, Bonnie Elosser, Chief Emenike, Tami & Winston Ely, Teena Fast, Keith Fowlkes, Frank Frey, Glenn and Bea Hill, Larry Hill, Dr. J.B. Hill, Betty Humphreys, Zafar Khan, David Kendall, Dana Kilgore, Jack Kennedy, Lanna Lumpkins, Valerie Lawson, Peggy Markham, Susan Mullins, Sara Love McReynolds, David and Gaynell Larsen, Rusty Necessary, Joe and Reba Smiddy, Gary Stratton, Ginger Vance, Roger and Beverly Viers, Bill Wendle, Debra Wharton, Dawneda Williams, Dr. Peter and Sandy Yun, Bob Adkins, Eliezer A. Alperstein, Gary Anderson, Kathleen Andres, Tony Herold, Jim Amos, Tracy Trost, Tom Pace, Cliff Michaels, Gregory Etherton, Wally Cato, S. Truett Cathy, Don Caudill, Ed Cerny, Christina Chia, Jerry Ho, Karen Cody, Linda Compton, Jim Connelly, Tom Cunningham, Seth Baker, Jarad Barr, Ernie Benko, Margo Berman, Shannon Blevins, Reed Bilbray, William Bone, James Brown, Jr., Raven Blair Davis, Rita Davenport, Shawn Davidson, Dirk Davis, Ron Dickenson, Greg Edwards, Louise Farley, Tom Gates, Valarie Gerlach, Marvin and Marcia Gilliam, Richard and Leslie Gilliam, Danny Greene, Bernetta Mullins, Jerry Greene, Toshiko Hartsock, Jeffery and Cindy Elkins, Sharon Ewing, Hasan Majied, Ida Holyfield, Lynda Hubbard, Brenda Salyers, James Humphreys, Hunter E. Craig, Sharon K. Jackson, Charlie and Jill Jessee, Alihan Karakarjal, Madeleine Kay, Patrick Kennedy, Bonnie

Kogos, Empress Dion Lawson, Lewey and Brenda Lee, Larry Levin, Steven and Loretta Levin, Cheri Lutton, Allyn Mark, Julia McAfee, Mark S. Mears, Alex Ong, Charlotte Parsons, Dr. Robert Patton, Joe D. Pippin, Don and Gigi Pippin, Gina Prince, Ed Primeau, Ricky Young, Jared Vasold, Jimmy Adkins, Jenay Tate, Katie Dunn, Jeff Lester, Phil Taylor, Joe Tennis, Adriana Trigiani, Markeda Wampler, Diane Ward, Jerry Wharton, Judith Williamson, Guang Chen "Alan", Uriel Martinez, Dr. William R. Wright, Donnie Ratliff, Jeremy Rayzor, Jon Reed, Greg Reid, Sharon Lechter, Ruby Rogers, Jon Schmitz, Ben and Nancy Sergent, Shin Saikyo, Ronnie and Marcia Shortt, Roger Sikorski, R.J. Sikorski, Zane Sturgill, Nancey Smith, Bonnie Solow, Lionel Sosa, Dr. Joe F. Smiddy, Ray Stendall, Toro Kawaguchi, Tatsuya Aminaka, Harai Kiyotaka, Cathy Still, William Sturgill, Ronald Sturgill, and Wendell and Brenda Barnette.

INTRODUCTION

———

MY VISION FOR YOU

I COULD NOT have written this book even a few years ago, because, as Henry David Thoreau wrote, "How vain it is to sit down to write when you have not stood up to live."

However, since I have been blessed to live a life that many people will only dream of, I write so that others may learn from this book—just as I have learned from others. Any financial gain from its publication will go 100 percent to college scholarships for needy individuals at the University of Virginia College at Wise, my own alma mater.

I am not trying to tell you some particular way to get rich, as there are literally thousands of ways to become financially secure if you have a passion and are willing to work hard, develop a plan or plans, involve others, and persist.

What I want to do is speak to you from experience so that you too can do what others before you have done if you repeat their actions, as long as this is your desire. Note that I said a desire that is so strong that it becomes a passion, not merely a wish.

To help the reader, perhaps I should tell you about myself. I am the son of a coal miner, and neither of my parents went beyond a grade-school education. Through my experience, I am going to show you that if you follow certain steps and principles, you can be a success.

My background is in finance and banking. At age 41, I became president and chief executive officer of a savings and loan that was on the verge of being closed by the federal banking authorities. The savings and loan had lost its capital of $1.5 million in the previous three years. The former CEO had not been able to keep the institution profitable; interest rates had gone out of sight, and there appeared to be no solution available. The savings and loan was located in a coal-mining area with a high rate of unemployment, a tremendous number of foreclosed properties, and loans with 30-year maturities at fixed rates that were much lower than the cost of deposits—not exactly an ideal situation. However, I was young, optimistic, and naïve.

For the next 18 years, while I was CEO, the savings and loan (later converted to a savings bank) was profitable every single year. In fact, it was very profitable. The bank was sold as I approached 60, and I was asked by the other trustees of the Napoleon Hill Foundation to become executive director and manage the foundation's affairs on a daily basis.

When I became executive director, I had little knowledge of book publishing, but my accounting degree, my years in banking, and my experience as owner of several businesses (in fields such as real estate development, dry cleaning services, commercial real estate rentals, cable television, and spring water) helped me tremendously. But in addition to having a varied business background, I have been a lover of books all my life. This love of books from a variety of varied disciplines had led me to read thousands of books and listen to hours upon hours of audiotapes.

Since I was a lover of books on success, including biographies, I became partial to Dr. Napoleon Hill because his works have endured for close to a century. Napoleon Hill's classic, *Think and Grow Rich!*, was first published in 1937. When I was in my twenties, I discovered *Think and Grow Rich!*, which had sold out its first printing in six weeks—even though it was priced at $2.50 in the middle of the Great Depression. This bestseller was reprinted three times in its first year. Today, first editions are offered for sale for $1,000 or more. It has been continuously in print for more than 70 years and still sells well. A recent survey of bestselling business books ranked *Think and Grow Rich!* as the number 15 motivational book of all time. Most such bestselling books disappear from the bookstores after 12 to 24 months, but continuous demand worldwide has made this one of the champion titles in history. *Think and Grow Rich!* has influenced millions of people. Motivational writers and speakers today will quickly tell you that they were deeply affected by the book.

There have been many books written about success, and you may wonder why another book should be written.

Some of the first books were those from people like Samuel Smiles, who wrote *Self-Help* in 1859. Smiles wrote about the human ability for self-improvement and wrote actual stories that showed persistence. Failure can be conquered by perseverance, and the many examples Smiles wrote about can be applied in today's world if success is your goal. Samuel Smiles's book was read and its principles absorbed by noted self-help authors such as Dr. Orison Swett Marden and Dr. Napoleon Hill. Both of these writers have been read by millions, especially Dr. Hill, the first self-help writer who studied more than 500 successful people in an attempt to answer the question, "Why are some people successful and others are not?"

Almost any book on self-help will give you another unique view, and if you remember learning your ABCs and multiplication tables, you no doubt did so by repetition. It is not likely that you can improve your station in life just by being exposed to self-help or inspirational literature, without continuous study of successful individuals.

The material for becoming a success is not complicated.

If you want to learn what other successful people have done, you can do so by looking at the material that is readily available. However, you need to always be aware of not just what the material is, but how you can use it to have a better life.

In a few minutes, I can show you how to become a millionaire without winning a lottery. But the problem is that about 98 out of 100 people lack *discipline*.

What I would like you to remember, whether you are reading this material or material from one of the other good writers today, is that it is not what you acquire or accomplish in your life that makes you successful. Becoming a millionaire or multimillionaire may engender a good feeling, and reaching any other worthwhile goal may be very satisfying to you, but the important point you should plant in your subconscious is that what you become during the process is what should matter most. When he wrote, "Success is a journey, not a destination," author Ben Sweetland probably said it best.

You should also note that the principles of success do not change.

The principles of the laws of attraction and sowing and reaping are as reliable as those of the law of gravity. When these principles are studied and applied, those who follow them can expect the same results that successful people have obtained. If you follow these principles, you can expect success, but when you violate them, you can expect failure.

What I desire for you is for you to become more than a millionaire.

The legacy that a person leaves behind should be something that made the world a better place in which to live.

Did you comfort the sick, clean up the environment, mentor the less fortunate, provide a scholarship, or help with a Boy or Girl Scout troop, or did you simply leave a lot of money to relatives who did little or nothing to deserve such an inheritance? The choice belongs to each of us, but my experience has taught me that *by far the happiest people are those who have made a positive impact upon the lives of others.*

These actions do not have to involve money; the person could as well have been a teacher, a guidance counselor, a law officer, or a member of any other honorable profession.

In the July 1921 edition of *Napoleon Hill's Magazine,* Napoleon Hill explained his use of the pronoun *I* and indicated that he was aware of the fact that a display of egotism can be seen as a weakness in a speaker or writer. But I am not trying to boost my ego when I use *I* to tell readers of my authentic experiences. These are not hypothetical experiences. When I am relating them, I am simply trying to inform you of them so that you can learn from them. I am telling them to you not to impress you, but to inspire you to pursue your goals and to lead an uncommon life.

1

THE FORMULA

You can do as much as you think you can,
But you'll never accomplish more;
And you can win, though you face the worst,
If you feel that you're going to do it.

—EDGAR A. GUEST

T HE GREATEST WASTE of all is the waste of our own potential mind power. The famous Harvard professor and psychologist William James estimated that the average person uses only 10 percent of his mental power. He has unlimited power—yet he uses only about one-tenth of it.

The power to be what you want to be, to get what you desire, and to accomplish whatever it is you are striving for abides within you. You are the one who is responsible for bringing it forth and putting it to work.

You can be whatever you make up your mind to be. Being happy, wealthy, or successful is a product of the mind and its unlimited possibilities.

Within you is this power that, when properly grasped and directed, can lift you out of the rut of mediocrity and place you among the few who make large accomplishments in life. You must learn to use this power and realize that the mind can achieve all things.

> One ship drives east and another drives west
> With the selfsame winds that blow.
> 'Tis the set of the sails, and not the gales,
> That tell us the way they go.
> Like the winds of the sea are the ways of fate,
> As we voyage along through life:
> 'Tis the set of a soul that decides its goal,
> And not the calm or the strife.
> —ELLA WHEELER WILCOX

Every sincere person wants to better her condition in life.

All wealth depends upon having a clear knowledge that the mind is the creator of wealth. You must control your thoughts if you are to control your circumstances.

If you are to obtain wealth, you must have the desire for wealth. Once you have this desire to create wealth, then you must achieve a belief that you can do it. If you believe that you can do it—see it as an existing fact—anything you can rightly wish for is yours. Belief is "the substance of things hoped for, the evidence of things not seen." This is why the saying "I will believe it when I see it" is incorrect—you will see it if you first believe it. The belief should come first.

One may observe that many people who have accomplished a great deal seem to be no more capable or learned than those who struggle day after day, yet accomplish very little. What is the power that gives new life to those who succeed on the road to success?

The power that makes accomplishments possible is belief. Belief or faith gives one the power to put forth the effort necessary to reach success and to avoid failure.

Your own belief in yourself is a power within you that makes all things attainable. You can do anything that you think you can do. Belief in yourself allows you the expectation that you can solve every problem that faces humanity and obtain everything that is right.

From the mind comes opportunity, with the only limitations being those that you place upon yourself.

Everything that can be desired is the result of thought.

William James said, "The more the mind does, the more it can do." Getting tired from doing is more a result of boredom than of fatigue from physical exertion.

You can work almost without ceasing when you are getting pleasure from your work.

If you are told repeatedly that you cannot do certain things, you may come to believe that you can't do them. Remember that success is a state of mind, but also remember that failure is a state of mind.

You must see yourself doing the thing you desire because you need to know that you can and will do it. The negative side of belief is that if you believe you cannot do a thing, you will not be able to do it.

It is necessary for you to believe in yourself if you are to make the most of your abilities. It is urgent that you believe in yourself in order to get others to cooperate with you in carrying out whatever tasks you are undertaking.

The only thing you have that will enable you to achieve success is your mind, and for your mind to perform at its best, you need to have a belief system with a spirit of optimism. You are not likely to perform well if you have a negative frame of mind. You cannot expect to create a positive outlook while you are holding on to negative thoughts. Fears, doubts, and other negative traits will diminish your dreams and aspirations in life. When Orison Swett Marden wrote that you must have castles in the air before you can have castles on the ground, he was saying that the thought of what you want to accomplish must be explicit in your mind before you can do it.

It is often easy to believe that the grass is greener on the other side, that you could be assured of success if only you could change your surroundings. The trouble with thinking that a change of environment would give you success is that true success comes from within.

Our inner thoughts bring either success or failure depending on which one we allow to dominate our thoughts.

The three words at the top of Chapter 1 of *Think and Grow Rich!* are "thoughts are things," and these words are very important if you desire success.

Your dominant thoughts make your inner world, and your outer world is but a reflection of your inner world.

Even if your past choices have been wrong because your thoughts have been negative, you can begin again because "our lives begin new at every sunrise." Richness is within, and no one has failed as long as she can try again. Only when one stops trying is one defeated.

You need only think, concentrate your thoughts on what you desire, and take the proper steps to make it possible for you to achieve your goals. The belief that achievement is possible will cause you to make the effort that is needed and to do it confidently.

Your mind will produce the necessary plans once you have the belief and begin. But this is where a large number of failures originate, because people fail to begin.

The successful people in this world have always been those who believed in themselves. This may seem like an impossible task, but remember that success comes from within, and that when you acquire this inner belief, it will be reflected in your physical or outer world. Believing and knowing are the necessary components of success. You must decide what is the most important thing you desire in your future. Always remember that you can be bold with your desires because the only limits are those that you place upon your mind. You should see what you desire, learn to visualize it, believe in it, and develop plans to achieve it.

Recently I spent the night in Charlotte, North Carolina, in order to have a meeting at 8 a.m. the following day concerning a publication project that the Napoleon Hill Foundation was involved in with a bestselling author and one of the most sought-after speakers in the United States. The author's name is Jeffrey Gitomer, and if you are not familiar with him, it would be wise for you to become so by visiting his website at www.gitomer.com.

The evening before my meeting, I went to a local restaurant and was waited on by a very nice waitress named Brooke. I told her that she would go places because of her outstanding personality. I also told her that at the office of the Napoleon Hill Foundation at the University of Virginia-Wise, a part-time employee, also named Brooke, had a good personality, and I bet they both were going places.

I told Brooke, "I bet you won't always be waiting on tables," and she said, "How did you know that waiting on tables is just a pit stop?" I thought, what a wonderful answer. I told her I noticed that young people who were working in jobs just to make some money, but looking ahead to a future once they have graduated from college, usually had a good attitude. People who work at low-wage jobs can easily develop the attitude that they are in a dead-end job. But if this applies to you, do what Brooke did: consider the low-paying job as a "pit stop," a temporary delay while you are getting ready for your future.

Have you ever believed that you can never be a millionaire because people who become rich have talents or other characteristics that people like you who are "average" don't have? When you have finished reading this book, if you still believe that the answer to this question is yes, then I have failed to get the truth across to you.

Success is truly a mind game, as my good friend Joe Dudley, Jr., realized. The circumstances of his early life would have given him plenty of excuses to fail.

In his book *Walking by Faith*, Joe lets the reader know that not only was he born into poverty in a large family, but he had a speech impediment and was labeled retarded. Also, being black was not exactly an asset when he was a child.

Dudley told 500 students at the annual Napoleon Hill Day held at the University of Virginia-Wise that his mother had explained to him that he might be slow, but that when he got something, he got it.

Did Joe ever get it? Today he owns the largest minority beauty cosmetic company in the United States. He is very wealthy, and he has given millions to worthy causes such as scholarships.

Once you have a purpose in your mind and you have a passion for it—or, as Napoleon Hill said, you have a "burning desire" to accomplish it—you are well on your way.

A task once begun is one-half done. Getting started is the most difficult part.

Once you have read, studied, and learned to believe the principles of success, you will have at your disposal the tools you need to overcome problems and to achieve personal growth that will enable you to take the success journey.

It is a person's aim or purpose that makes her. Without aim, she is like tumbleweed in that it is the wind that determines where she goes. Let one obstacle get in her way, and if she has no aim or purpose, she will alter her path. She focuses on her weakness, misery, and failure—in other words: "My life is aimless."

A well-ascertained and generous purpose gives vigor, direction, and perseverance to all of a person's life.

The qualities associated with a strong purpose are a well-disciplined intellect, character, influence, tranquility, and cheerfulness within—and those are what lead to success. Whatever a person's talents and advantages may be, if he has no aim or a low one, he will be weak and despicable; if he has a high purpose, he cannot be other than respectable and influential. Without some definite object before us, some standard that we are earnestly striving to reach, we cannot expect to attain any great height, either mentally or morally. But setting high standards for ourselves and wishing to reach them without any further effort on our part is not enough to elevate us to any great degree.

It has been said, "Nature holds for each of us all that we need to make us useful and happy; but she requires us to labor and wait for all we get." We are given nothing of value that does not include the need for labor; and we can expect to overcome difficulties only by strong and noble work. In our striving for "something better than we have known," we should work for others' good rather than for our own pleasure. Those whose object in life is their own happiness find at last that their lives are sad failures.

We each need to do something each day that moves us worthily in the direction of our definite plan of action. More than just dreaming is necessary if we are to succeed in the objects and ambitions of our life. We achieve our best results in every department of life only when we thoughtfully plan and earnestly work in the proper directions.

Purposes without action are dead. Work is necessary, and it is vain to hope for good results without good plans. Random or half-hearted efforts are generally only a waste of time.

Successful people's purpose in life always involves careful plans followed by action.

Whether the object is learning or wealth, the ways and means are always laid out according to the best plans and methods. A sea captain uses a chart; an architect, plans; and a sculptor, a model—and all of them use these tools as a way to success. Even great inspirations that may be defined as genius can do little unless they include action applied to a well-formed plan; when they do, every step is a move toward the accomplishment of the chief aim or purpose in one's life. No effort or time is lost, for nothing is done at random.

In the grand aim of life, some worthy purpose should be kept constantly in view, and every effort to accomplish it must be made every day. If you do that, you will, perhaps unconsciously, approach the goal of your ambition.

There should be no question that fixedness of purpose is the greatest element of human success.

When a person has formed a great sovereign purpose in her mind, it governs her conduct just as the laws of nature, such as the law of gravity, govern the operation of physical things.

Everyone who is interested in success should have an aim in view, and should pursue it steadily. She should not be distracted from her route by other objects that come into her view, even though they may appear to be highly attractive. People do not live long enough to accomplish everything. Indeed, only a few can accomplish more than one thing well. Many people accomplish nothing worthwhile.

Yet there is not a person who is endowed with ordinary intellect who cannot accomplish at least one useful, important, worthy purpose. Some of those whom history rates as among the greatest of men were trained from youth to choose some definite object in life, to which they directed all their thoughts and all their energy.

It became the sole purpose of their hearts and was the basis for their future accomplishments.

If you are to be successful, it is not enough just to dream of success. It is not enough just to believe that you can be successful. You must develop your own set of goals defining what becoming a success means to you. It could be that your idea of being successful is simply to make a certain amount of money. Only you can determine what your goals are to be, and it is reaching those goals that you determine that will make you a success.

However, once you have made that amount of money, you may find yourself asking, "Is that all there is to life?" That is why you need to include plans to help others who have been less fortunate. Someone once said that statues and other honors are never given for what someone does for himself, but for what he has done for others.

Just what are the factors that define what it takes to be a success? If you ask different people, you will receive many different answers. Some will suggest being highly educated; others will think it takes hard work. Others will remember President Calvin Coolidge's statement on persistence. Walter Chrysler, the automobile genius, reminded us that nothing worthwhile was ever accomplished without enthusiasm. All of these traits are of great help, but by themselves they are not what it takes to make someone successful.

For example, education enables people's accomplishments, but getting an education does not assure one's success. The world is full of educated people who do not realize that knowledge is important only when it is applied.

Hard work is a good trait, but untold numbers of people have worked hard, long hours for years but never seen success.

Factors that determine success are offering a service or a product that is desired in the market.

Note that I did not say a service or product that people need. Ray Kroc made millions by selling hamburgers; this was not necessarily a product that people needed, but it was something they wanted. The degree to which you do something better than others and receive just rewards for your service or product will determine your success.

Qualities such as persistence, working hard, and having integrity are all important if you are to succeed. Yet all of these will not assure your success.

The first step to success begins in our thought process. When Napoleon Hill put the three words "Thoughts are things" at the beginning of the all-time bestseller *Think and Grow Rich!* in 1937, he was stating an essential fact of the success process that he had discovered during his 20 years of research.

Thoughts truly are things, but it is important that the thought process concentrate on a purpose that will supply a human want and at the same time be something for which you have a deep passion. The reason passion is important is that even when you have a wonderful idea, if you do not have passion, you are likely to quit when the going gets tough. Passion will make you want to persist, seek other plans when they are needed, get help from others, or, in other words, stick with your goal until it is accomplished.

As mentioned before, the first step to success takes place in your thought process, and the way in which we use it is extremely important for our success.

If you study the thought process, you will realize that we think in pictures, and that the more vividly we think in pictures, the more these mental pictures aid us on the road to success. The brilliant ancient thinker Aristotle said, "It is impossible even to think without a mental picture." Think of mental pictures as a movie playing inside your mind.

Once you have a mental picture of what you wish to accomplish, you must commit yourself to acquiring whatever is lacking if you are to reach your destination. Determining what you wish to accomplish is absolutely a necessity to make your mental pictures a reality.

Once you have selected your goal or purpose and have committed to it, you must formulate plans. You must then put those plans into action. Many people have good mental pictures and may even have plans, but until you take action, nothing happens.

You cannot just think, dream, or wish for something to happen; you must take action.

Even if your plans prove to be inadequate, you must begin because you can always alter your plans, or even get new plans. Very seldom will you have all the answers in the beginning. When it seems that after your first, second, or later attempt, you have not succeeded, remember Thomas Edison's attempts to find a filament that would not burn out so fast; he made more than 10,000 attempts before being successful.

Look at each attempt that you complete not as a failure, but as an education.

What you wish to accomplish in the marketplace should focus on the necessary improvements—such as better service, improved quality, better price, or some other quality—for which would-be buyers will be willing to pay a price that will give you a satisfactory profit.

Several years ago, I was part of a group that had the idea of forming a cable television company. Cable television had become very popular, but building a new cablevision company would be a challenge. The process was an "overbuild." In other words, we were planning to build a new cable television network in towns where cable television was already well established. It was obvious that in order to get consumers to change to our new cable television network, we had to offer a better deal—to offer a price that would be much lower, yet still give us an adequate return on our investment.

We realized that most other cable television companies had large debts resulting from the purchase of expensive equipment and the use of costly labor; they then had to pay the interest on that huge debt load, and also needed to give the shareholders a return on their investments. In addition, being a publicly traded company usually means that your accounting and legal fees are higher.

Among its founders, our cable company had myself (a bank president), a CPA, and an attorney. In the beginning, we decided that we would not borrow any money, but that each of us would contribute the amount necessary, and thus the company would have no debt. At once our new company had costs that were much lower than those of most other cable companies. This "no debt" feature allowed us to make the monthly cable fee much lower, which met the criterion of providing a product and service that was appealing to consumers.

The group was truly a mastermind alliance, because each investor had the same goal, which was making a good return on our investment. Each member had a particular wealth of knowledge to offer the company, thus greatly increasing the likelihood that the venture would be a success.

After about eight years, our cable company was sold to a large cable company for cash. The idea had matured into a very successful undertaking.

It is what you become during your journey that is most important.

Your plans are like a road map, showing you the steps you are to take. Your plans often get changed, but that only means that you try other steps, change direction, or do whatever else is necessary. If where you want to go is important, keep on trying. I would even suggest that you keep a reminder handy.

Napoleon Hill, in his lectures, often asked his audience how many times the average person tried a task before quitting. Often those in attendance would answer one, two, or three. Hill would reply that the average was less than one, because many people never start.

W. Clement Stone, the founder of Combined Insurance (now AON) started with $100 and grew it to an empire worth several hundred million. He was noted for saying, "Just do it!"

I remember often hearing Mr. Stone, who was the chairman of the Napoleon Hill Foundation at the time, listening to a board member and then remarking, "Just do it." He gave away thousands of buttons (I still have mine) that say simply, "Just Do It."

> *We become like those with whom we associate: a mirror reflects a man's face, but what he is really like is shown by the kind of friends he chooses.*
>
> — PROVERBS 27:19

Here's another important idea: get others to help you make progress.

In my 38 years in finance, the number of horror stories I heard would fill a book. While this is not a book about real estate, just remember that real estate has been one of the areas where many millionaires made their money.

You cannot expect to be an expert on all topics. Recall the story of Andrew Carnegie, the founder of what became U.S. Steel. Carnegie needed accountants, lawyers, chemists, marketing people, and experts in other areas in which he lacked knowledge. While Carnegie did not know all the answers in steelmaking, he knew enough to select people who could help him become extremely wealthy.

More than once, I had people come to the bank looking for a real estate loan. Once the application was completed, the bank would obtain credit information to determine whether the applicant paid her bills and had the ability to repay the loan. The next step would be to get a dependable licensed appraiser to determine the value of the real estate. This is basically done by comparing the property with other comparable properties in the area that have recently been sold. If the credit, income, and appraisal are in order, a certified survey is obtained.

The next step is to get an attorney to do an abstract of the property to verify ownership, taxes, and any liens that were "attached" to the property. Judgments, tax liens, and other deeds of trust would have to be paid first should the property go into foreclosure for nonpayment. Next, the attorney would be instructed to obtain title insurance to ensure that the real estate that the bank is making a loan on is free and clear of any claims.

Many times, I met people who had a deed on which taxes were outstanding or judgments had been filed, and even situations in which previous owners had failed to get all the parties involved to sign away their interest before conveying the property.

I saw people use their own money or even borrow from a bank to build a house without obtaining a survey, only to discover later that the house had been partially or completely built on someone else's property, or did not have a right of way from a public street to their property. This would not have happened if they had had a survey.

Whether you are buying real estate or starting a business, a good attorney is an absolute necessity. Hiring an attorney to prevent mistakes will cost you a lot less money and time than having to hire an attorney to correct mistakes that could have been prevented.

Robert "Bob" Johnson Jr., who has been the Napoleon Hill Foundation's attorney, is an expert in copyright law. Bob worked for many years for a very prestigious law firm in Chicago and took early retirement to do the foundation's work so that he could slow down a little from the hectic pace of his required travel and hours. The foundation gets hundreds of questions on a regular basis, and Bob's expertise saves us untold hours of work and prevents problems on a daily basis.

Don't gamble when you are unsure; get the help of experts, and you will save money and time by lessening the number of errors committed.

Don't be afraid to ask, because you never know what help you may get if you try.

I once started a book project that took me two years to complete and get a publisher. I will relate only the part of the book deal that was obtained by asking. The book, sponsored by the Napoleon Hill Foundation, was based on the story from *Think and Grow Rich!* of R. U. Darby, where Darby quit three feet from a rich vein of gold.

My book was focused from the start on interviews with notables of today, asking them the question, "When things were tough in your life, why did you not give up?" The book was begun when the economy was in a serious downturn, and this reminded me that Napoleon Hill wrote his classic *Think and Grow Rich!* during the Great Depression. My manuscript was submitted to various publishers with Greg S. Reid as the author, but it did not draw the interest that I had expected. It needed more depth and polish.

I called Sharon L. Lechter and asked her if she would be interested in helping on the project. I knew that Sharon was very capable and that her expertise would add value to the book.

Sharon was the coauthor of 14 *Rich Dad, Poor Dad* books that have sold 27 million copies in over 50 countries. She was a Certified Public Accountant and a member of the President's Advisory Council on Financial Literacy, and she had marketing experience that would prove invaluable in selling the book. Sharon said yes, because she was working on financial literacy with the Napoleon Hill Foundation and was very proud of the association.

Once the manuscript was completed, a contract could have been signed with several publishers, but I suggested a certain publisher, and Sharon and Greg agreed. The reason for the selection of this particular publisher was its apparent willingness to support the book to make it a bestseller. Getting into position to get the tremendous support needed was done by asking for a meeting with the CEO of the bookselling chain that owned the publishing company.

When the publisher was asked to arrange a meeting, he remarked that it was not customary for the company head to meet with authors, but he made the request anyway. The answer was yes, but that we should not expect more than five minutes of the chief executive's time.

In fact, the chief executive didn't give us just five minutes, he gave us more than an hour to pitch the book. Not only did he give us tremendous support, but he told his sales staff that if they had ever promoted a book, they should do so with *Three Feet from Gold*, and that he wanted our next project.

After the contract was signed, the next step was promotion. Between the authors and the Napoleon Hill Foundation, we enlisted literally thousands of friends, and every single one who was asked to assist gladly did so. Some sent e-mails or posted on their websites, or on Facebook, Twitter, or other sites. Some of the most respected leaders in the publishing industry, such as Bob Proctor, Harvey Ecker, Mark Victor Hansen, Les Brown, John Gray, and Mark Sanford, made appearances to promote the book. All this support was given simply for the asking, with no monetary consideration.

By now I hope you realize that you can greatly improve your results by simply asking those who are in a position to help to do so. Often, the most successful people in their respective professions will also be the most accessible and willing to assist others. If you remember any advice that you may have received in this book, it is, "You give to get."

The final results of all the questions asked and the help given was *Three Feet from Gold* making the bestseller list at Amazon and Barnes & Noble the first week it was available. In the United States, about 200,000 books are printed each year, and only about 15,000 ever make it to the shelves of the major bookstores.

Don't ever be afraid to ask for help; otherwise you are not likely to reach the degree of success that can be achieved with the right associations.

In a speech that President Ronald Reagan gave shortly after the attempt on his life, he quoted poet Carl Sandburg: "The republic is a dream. Nothing happens unless first a dream." Reagan then went on to say, "And that's what makes us, as Americans, different. We've always reached for a new spirit and aimed at a higher goal."

Who would not like to be successful?

But first, each person needs to define what success means to him as an individual. If you were born in an environment of poverty, it would be natural to put a strong emphasis on money. So if you develop a belief that success is defined by the amount of money you can acquire, you will be likely to believe that the more money you acquire, the more successful you are.

If the pursuit of happiness becomes your goal, you will probably discover that wealth as measured by money does not ensure happiness. The other side of the equation is that poverty does not guarantee happiness either.

Many people, just as I did, put a lot of emphasis on acquiring money while they are young, but later discover that their emphasis has changed. Early on, it is likely to be a desire to make money to satisfy their needs and wants.

Hopefully, as you mature in life, you will realize that money is simply a tool that can be exchanged for goods or services. Money can be used for worthy projects, whether those projects are funding scholarships, teaching to help overcome financial illiteracy, fighting poverty, or thousands of other things that can help the disadvantaged and truly make the world a better place in which to live.

If you are going to be successful, which I assume you intend to be, then even if you do not realize it yet, a definite purpose is the starting point. If you do not have a definite purpose, you can be best described as a drifter. Drifting through life does not make one successful. Through studying successful people for over 45 years, I have found that all successful people had in mind where they were going. Once they knew where they were going, they made plans, changed them if necessary, got help when the expertise of others was needed, and persisted until they achieved their goals.

There are several reasons why having a purpose in mind will help you succeed. For one thing, what you decide upon will bring about the need to study—and you can become an expert. Once you have acquired specialized education, you will be rewarded with appropriate work and opportunity.

Once you have determined your particular interest, you will attract opportunities to yourself and attract other people who can assist you.

When someone says that like attracts like, it simply means that success attracts success and poverty attracts poverty. Put simply, as one might tell a young person associating with questionable friends, birds of a feather flock together.

Remember these points and, more important, apply them, and you will develop a belief in yourself that will enhance your success. If others have been successful, why can't you be? The choice is yours and yours alone.

It has been noted that we make a living by what we get and a life by what we give.

2

SUCCESS

Always bear in mind that your own resolution to
succeed is more important than any one thing.
—ABRAHAM LINCOLN

I F YOU WISH to be successful, here are the steps that will help you get there. You can read scores of books on the subject, or you can follow these simple steps and take action.

If you are to improve your station in life, positive change must take place. Here are five things you need to do:

1. Have a desire to improve. You can refer to this as your ultimate goal, your mission, your purpose, or something else, but it must be a burning obsession or passion. It must be so strong that you live it, eat it, go to bed with it, and are consumed by the need to "see" it materialize.

2. Belief is a state of mind that lets you be confident that your purpose will come alive. This can be achieved by often-repeated affirmations that make it a part of your subconscious. You should have notes or signs placed where you can see them daily as constant reminders of your purpose.

3. You generate actions based on the belief that you can accomplish your purpose in life. Action leads to practice. Perfect practice makes for perfection.

4. Feedback is what you get as a result of taking action. If the feedback is negative, such as falling when you are learning to ski, then you should accept it as a lesson, not a failure. The fall just means that you need more practice, maybe with the help of a professional instructor.

5. Repetition means doing the action over and over until the right results become a habit.

**With discipline, we make our habits,
then our habits make us.**

Of course there will be temporary setbacks, but remember that if a child who is learning to walk quit as soon as most adults do, the child would never learn to walk. I learned that either I could follow these steps taken by other successful people to get what I wanted, or I would have to make excuses for why I did not. It all sounds simple, and in fact it is easy, but delaying these steps is also easy. If you are not ready to study and apply what other success stories tell you, then you should be prepared to make excuses.

Remember the saying that success requires no explanation, while failure requires alibis.

When I was still a teenager, my "place of business" was called the Indian Mountain Reptile Garden. The center of the enterprise was the "snake pit," which held as many as 100 poisonous snakes. The snakes that were native to the mountains of southwestern Virginia were the timber rattlesnake and the copperhead. I began to add some other animals in small cages to the area behind the snake pit—Tom the bobcat, Stinky the skunk, an albino groundhog, peacocks, and other exotic birds. A little later, I purchased three small monkeys.

On August 13, 2009, the *Coalfield Progress* ran the following item in a column on local history 50 years earlier, August 13, 1959, "Eighteen-year-old Donald Green, a husky young man who planned to attend Clinch Valley College in the fall, was making a living operating the Indian Mountain Reptile Garden, a tourist attraction centered on snakes. Other animals at the little zoo included two bobcats, an albino groundhog, tufted chickens, a flying squirrel and a South American monkey."

Below is the full article that appeared in August 13, 1959, where the headline read, "Snakes Are Big Tourist Attraction in Wise County."

Well, snakes alive!!
There are an awful lot of people, both in and out of Wise county, who can't stand the sight of any kind of snake, but there's one young man, up on Indian Creek Mountain, on the Wise-Pound road, who makes a pretty decent living, depending solely upon the so-called "slimy critters."

Eighteen year old Donald Green, a husky young man, who is planning to attend Clinch Valley College, this Fall, is the operator of the Indian Mountain Reptile Garden— and seems to enjoy his work.

Green's weird occupation began five summers ago, when he and two friends were discussing the idea of a tourist attraction. Green mentioned that quite a few "snake gardens" were in existence in Florida, and the trio started mulling over the possible advantages of erecting such an enterprise, in Wise county.

Finally, the group decided to try their luck, and the erection of Indian Mountain Reptile Garden was begun. Soon, the six foot-deep reptile pit, and the adjoining souvenir stand, were complete, except for one little detail—no snakes!

The problem was easily solved. The boys secured the services of Vic Bates of Wise, who has reportedly been catching snakes for the past 16 years, and journeyed to High Knob, near Norton, for a snake hunting expedition.

"We had pretty good luck, on our first trip," says Green. "We got plenty of rattlesnakes, and a few copperheads, right away, without much trouble."

So, with the building completed, and the snakes ready to be put in the pit, the boys were open for business. But not unlike every good establishment, the youths soon decided to expand their investment, by ordering four diamond-back rattlers from Texas.

"The rattlers were shipped into Norton by freight," Green explains, "and I think that's the most expensive freight anybody could ever order."

The Texas reptiles were placed in the cinder-block pit, along with the Virginia critters, and Green's business began to boom.

But Green's mind could not be at ease, until the reptile garden was expanded again. Cages were built, at the rear of the snake pit, and he began plans to secure other animals, other than his snakes.

A South American monkey was shipped to Wise county, and became Green's pride and joy. More animals were purchased, until at present, the miniature zoo contains two bobcats, an albino groundhog, tufted chickens, and a flying squirrel.

(Flying squirrels do not actually fly, explains Green. "They have webs, between the body and forearms, but to be correct, they soar, not fly.")

But a job managing a reptile garden does present some problems, according to Green. "Snakes in captivity do not eat," he says, "but only bite and kill the rats and mice, which I put in the pit." He adds that a new supply of snakes is needed every year, because the captive reptiles starve themselves to death.

And the tourist business is still booming, Green says.

"I've seen cars from about every state in the U.S., stopping here, during the last couple summers," he boasts.

So, next time you're fishing, or on a picnic, and see a snake basking in the sun, think twice before running— it may be the beginning of a new and interesting occupation.

The purchase I made that I was proudest of was a small black bear that had been captured by Indians that I bought out of state for $100. My dad, a coal miner, borrowed a truck from a fellow worker and hauled the bear to the "snake pit," where a cage had been constructed. I named the little bear Sammy, not knowing whether it was male or female. Sammy was in a large cage about 14 × 14, but with sleeping quarters that he could enter through an opening.

My father was a repairman in underground coal mines, and he understood electricity. He installed heat lamps in the sleeping quarters for Sammy the bear and Buck the big stump-tailed monkey.

Sammy was quite an attraction. Many of the paying customers had never seen a live bear before. I was still in high school, but I had a little gold mine. First, the snakes were an attraction, and many people would visit several times during the summer. I rented a soft drink machine and started selling snacks, then I added souvenirs: imprinted postcards, flags, and other novelties that had very high profit margins.

By the time I was a senior in high school, I had very few fears (which was probably naïve), and Sammy had grown up fast. As part of my routine, I would feed the animals before I went to school. Often I would go into Sammy's cage and play with him. Sammy would get on his hind legs and put his paws on my shoulders. Sometimes I would push him to the floor, and he would bounce back up. After a few minutes, however, he would get rough, and I would leave the cage quickly.

One day while I was in class, someone from the principal's office called the room over the public address system and said, "If Don Green is in class, tell him his mother called and said that his black bear had got out of his cage and his mother said for him to come home."

It probably took me about 15 minutes to get home and discover a lot of excitement. No doubt when I had left the cage that morning, I had closed the cage door, but had failed to lock it. Sometime during the day, Sammy had pushed against the door; since it was not locked, it came open, and Sammy had his freedom. The bear was going wild, running around and chasing the ducks (he killed one of them), and the monkeys in their cages were screaming and making noises I had never heard before.

Mom was scared half to death and probably had an urge to have me put away somewhere. My mom is now 89, but she remembers vividly the details of the time when my bear named Sammy escaped.

While this happened years ago, I still remember it well. I was not the least bit excited, and I really enjoyed what was happening. I did not see the potential danger that a black bear could easily kill a person. Monroe Moore, a bread salesman, had stopped (along with a lot of traffic). At once I got the idea of getting a box of oatmeal cakes from the salesman, as I remembered that Sammy loved sweets. When Sammy saw me, he realized that I had something for him. So I started unwrapping a cake and pitched it toward him. At the same time, I was backing up toward Sammy's bear cage. By the time I got Sammy close to the door, I had one cake left, and I pitched it barely inside the door.

Sammy realized what was happening, and he stuck his head in the door to get the cake and started to back out. I took my foot and kicked his butt; it caused him to jump forward, and I closed the door. This time I locked the door and went back to school.

You may wonder how this story is related to the book. Here's how.

Sometimes force, coercion, threats, and intimidation may work, but giving someone something that he wants or needs will usually get better and longer-lasting results. The old saying is, one can catch more flies with honey than with vinegar.

This lesson applies even more to people: you are much more likely to get what you want by helping others get what they either need or want. When you work with others and apply the Golden Rule, you will be rewarded. It has been said that you can never exercise any great amount of influence over others until you first learn to exercise control over yourself.

SUCCESS

Nobody can define success for someone else, but the desire to be successful is the starting point for everyone.

Success should bring you personal contentment with your own life while you strive to make the world a better place in which to live. A personal commitment to do something that you have a passion for will help you to develop a life that truly matters.

James A. Brown, Jr., gave me my first job in banking, and I remember the interview as if it were today. "Jim" told me, "If you do a little extra for a day or for a week, it might not matter, but over a period of years, it will separate you from the rest, who will only dream of success."

Often you can find yourself in a position where you can help someone in a way that can deeply affect her life and the lives of others for eternity.

While I was president of the bank, some of the employees asked me to consider giving a job to a young lady named Janet. She had had a tragedy in her family that it would be difficult to even imagine. She was an excellent employee and had a wonderful attitude, but some days she would recall her tragedy, and it was tough for her emotionally.

One day Janet said to me, "You know, I would love to teach young children, but it would take me a long time to finish and get my degree." I asked her how long it would take, and she said three years. I asked her, "How old will you be in three years if you don't go to school?" She started laughing, and I saw to it that every course she took was paid for in advance. Janet has been teaching young children and teaching music, which she absolutely loves, for several years.

Not only had she been an excellent employee, but recently I was more than rewarded for helping her. Janet called the Napoleon Hill Foundation office and asked if she could come by because she wanted me to meet Andy, her son-in-law, who had recently returned from his second tour with the Marine Corps. in Iraq. While they were in my office, Janet recalled the story about how she got to return to college. Today Janet is having a wonderful impact on young people's lives.

If you have not discovered this yet, hopefully you will find that life's best rewards are not monetary in nature.

3

ADVERSITY AND FAILURE

You gain strength, courage and confidence by
every experience in which you really stop to look
fear in the face. You are able to say to yourself,
"I have lived through this horror. I can take the
next thing that comes along." You must do the
thing you think you cannot do.

— ELEANOR ROOSEVELT

OVERCOMING ADVERSITY IS akin to reaching a goal. To get past adversity or reach a goal, you need not know all the answers before you start your mission. But you do need to have a clear view of what your goal is or a clear view of the problem you are facing. At this juncture, the most important thing is to be on the right course.

To begin to solve a problem or reach a goal, you first must determine what you want in your future. Albert Einstein said, "In the middle of difficulty lies opportunity."

You should always remember that while you may know what you want and have a good idea of how to get it, unless you are inspired to put forth the necessary effort, you will not be a success.

However, once you raise your desire to a burning passion, you will find the means to accomplish what you want. You will not have all the answers, but you will accumulate answers and assistance from others once you are inspired enough to start your journey to success.

People who are successful used what they knew when they started plus the knowledge that they acquired on their voyage. Inspiration kept them going even when obstacles got in their way.

In Victor Frankl's milestone book *Man's Search for Meaning*, about his confinement in the Nazi death camp at Auschwitz, Frankl said that he discovered that man would find a how once he had a why. This is like a goal or obstacle that will be met with success or overcome once the why is developed into a passion or a burning desire to overcome whatever may lie in one's path to success.

Winston Churchill put it well when he said, "Success is going from failure to failure without loss of enthusiasm."

This is the reason why many people start for a specified destination and do not quit until they reach that destination. Those who know their destination and have a strong desire to reach it will not stop until they do so. Also, there is one main reason why many people fail: they do not get started. Either they simply do not begin or they start, but are stopped by the slightest obstacle in their path.

As writer Frank Clark put it, "If you can find a path that has no obstacles, it probably doesn't lead anywhere." Your journey is not likely to be smooth, but you will learn from your failures—sometimes even more than from your successes.

While you are on your journey, remember that each of us should make the world a better place in which to live. Progress has always been a result of each generation's desire to make the world a better place for the generation that follows.

> *Adversity is the diamond dust Heaven polishes its*
> *jewels with.*
>
> —THOMAS CARLYLE

You will learn sooner or later that we promote our own happiness to the exact degree that we contribute to the comfort and happiness of others.

To overcome obstacles and hardships, steadiness in one's progress and a determination to succeed must always be present. Remember what writer Elbert Hubbard said, "The greatest mistake you can make in life is to be continually fearing that you will make one."

If you give up easily, become disenchanted when your goals are blocked, and think that you must wait until all conditions are favorable and your progress appears easy, you will be very unlikely to go far in today's fast-paced world. Circumstances will probably never be such that success is assured, and there will never be a time when all conditions are ideal, and the reason most people never succeed is that they wait for perfect circumstances.

Obstacles are not there to block one's path, but to be used as stepping-stones on the path of life.

Also, the very struggle to overcome the obstacles that hinder your progress will serve to make you stronger while you pursue your goals. As the writer John Neal so aptly stated, "A certain amount of opposition is a great help to a man. Kites rise against, not with, the wind."

That Old Witch—Bad Luck

> *What is the thought that is in your mind?*
> *Is fear ever running through it?*
> *If so, just tackle the next you find*
> *By thinking you're going to do it.*
>
> —EDGAR A. GUEST

If you face misfortune and so-called bad luck, and you always seem to be in the wrong place at the wrong time, then you fall into the company of many other people.

If this is where you find yourself, you need to learn fast that *you* are the cause of all the trouble that is besetting you.

Fear is simply a result of creative thought, but while creative thought is useful, it is useful only in the positive form. Negative creative thinking creates fear.

In the Bible, we read of Job, who stated, "The thing which I greatly feared is come upon me."

Panic and fear do not develop unless our thought processes are negative.

An example of the thought process and what it can do to you: Shakespeare said, "There is nothing either good or bad, but thinking makes it so."

Even when you have challenges to deal with or difficulties to overcome, there is nothing to be afraid of. Things that happen are effects of your mental process. You need to concentrate only on good things and the things you desire. Any negative thoughts or worries about poverty or sickness should be removed from your mind.

Each of us has had successes and failures. Let the failures be lessons learned, but don't dwell on them because you can hold onto the past so tightly that you don't take the time to embrace the future.

Sir Edmund Hillary, the mountain climber, wrote, "It is not the mountain we conquer but ourselves."

If you must spend time thinking about the past, recall your successes, no matter how small they may appear to you. Previous successes encourage you to be persistent.

You should become energized by studying the lives of people who have overcome adversity, whether the people were famous or not.

The lives of others can be an inspiration and can demonstrate to each of us that examples are usually a great benefit to us in learning what we can accomplish. Novelist Henry Fielding noted, wisely, "Adversity is the trial of principle. Without it a man hardly knows whether he is honest or not."

Your chances of being a success will be limited if you are so afraid of success that you will not attempt to overcome challenges and adopt new ideas to climb the ladder of success.

It was Alexander Graham Bell who reminded us, "When one door closes another opens; but we often look so long and so regretfully upon the closed door that we do not see the one which has opened for us."

If, as a small child, we quit trying to walk the first time we fell down, we would never learn to walk. We need to repeat our attempts over and over, whether we are learning to walk or memorizing our ABCs or our multiplication tables, until we can perform the task almost without thinking.

Parents realize when a child is small that learning to walk and learning the ABCs and the multiplication tables takes time and must be repeated many times before the tasks can be performed almost without effort.

But as a child grows, the parents often want to protect him from injury, embarrassment, or other things that the parent feels are against the child's best interest. They give such advice as, "Don't go in the water until you learn to swim" or "Don't cross the street." As the child gets older, his desire for an education at a top-rated college can be damaged by a statement like, "Only rich parents can send their children to schools like that." Parents who mean well can so damage a child's ambition by negative statements that the child will not attempt to do what would be best for his future.

The only thing we have to fear is fear itself.
— FRANKLIN D. ROOSEVELT

Fear takes away your strength and breeds inaction, which means that even if you have ideas and plans, you will not take the necessary steps to accomplish your goals.

Most of the fears that we let dominate our lives have no justification or basis in fact.

The little things we know that we use to allow fear to set in simply do not stand up when the information is analyzed. Many different studies show that about 60 to 70 percent of the things we fear never happen. Thus, our fears are mostly without basis.

These studies regarding fear report that about 5 percent of all fears have a valid basis and thus are justified. This means that the other 95 percent of fears involve either things from the past over which we have no control or unimportant items that are of little concern and will make very little difference.

If 5 percent of our fears are things that we should not ignore, we should still work on achieving our goals.

Goals give us energy, and while we do not always respond to reason, taking action will help us eliminate the fears that we have developed. Staying focused on your goal will keep you positive, and while the mind is complicated, it cannot hold negative and positive thoughts at the same time.

It also is important for you to focus on those items that you can control and learn to ignore what you cannot control.

**Facing fear and overcoming your fears, even
if small, will give you confidence and help
you face up to fears in the future.**

An example is the fear of public speaking, which to many people is greater than the fear of death. Once a person speaks in public, her confidence increases with each speech.

The danger is that if we do not acknowledge our fears and take action, those fears can make us inactive, and we will become failures in life.

When I was a teenager, I went with some adults and learned to capture poisonous snakes, most of which were rattlesnakes. People in general have a tremendous fear of snakes. However, most snakes are not poisonous, and there is no reason to be afraid of them. For example, in the mountains of Virginia, where I live, there are only two types of poisonous snakes, timber rattlesnakes and copperheads. Just as about 95 percent of our fears have no basis, there is no reason for the observer to fear any of the other snakes.

As with other fears, if you study snakes and get to know the ones that are dangerous, you can remove the fear. In addition, poisonous snakes will bite when they are threatened, but if they are given space, they will retreat. The best protection is knowledge and realizing that poisonous snakes cannot strike you successfully if you maintain a distance between yourself and the snake of at least the length of the snake.

The reason I overcame any fear of poisonous snakes was that I was motivated by money. As discussed in the previous chapter, I exhibited the snakes in a snake pit, and viewers paid admission to look at them. On good days, I often made $100, and in the 1950s, that was a tremendous amount of money to a teenager. The fact that I had earned the money made it much more satisfying than it would have been if it had been a gift.

Most of our fears have very little basis. Remember, the issue is not so much what happens to us as to how we respond to what has happened.

When children grow up in a home with alcoholic parents, some will choose to be nondrinkers, while others will become alcoholics. The two groups had the same background, but completely opposite reactions to it. However, failure can serve a purpose because it can give us the chance to learn something.

We will never meet anyone who has not made mistakes in the past. Successful people learn from failure, while unsuccessful people accept failure and quit trying.

Each attempt we make to succeed brings with it the possibility of failing, but you simply cannot achieve success in life without accepting the fact that failure simply means you have the chance to try another plan.

One thing that happened during those "snake pit" days was that a customer paid me with a silver dollar. The customer was from Ohio, and I vividly recall that day because I still have that silver dollar. As coin collecting is a hobby of mine, I have been the owner of thousands of U.S. silver dollars, but I scratched "Phyl" on the face of this particular one (not a particularly smart idea). Phyl was my girlfriend as a teenager and is now my wife and the mother of my beautiful daughter, Donna.

Remember that if fears invade your mind and remain there, they will put a brake on your movement toward achievement.

Many people let negative thinking affect the decisions they make and the actions they take or fail to take. Negative people choose to remain in a comfort zone, although they would have a greater chance of success if they used positive thoughts to remove their fears and take action.

It was President Dwight D. Eisenhower who said, "One can attain a high degree of security in a prison cell if that's all he wants out of life." To be successful and achieve your desired goal, you must take risks.

"Many of life's failures are people who did not realize how close they were to success when they gave up." This statement was made by Thomas Edison, probably the most noted inventor the world has ever known.

FAILURE

Something is a failure if it leads you to quit—whether it be after one attempt or one hundred attempts to accomplish something worthwhile.

There are many things in history that could have been called failure, such as Thomas Edison and the lightbulb. After 10,000 attempts, Edison simply continued to look at each attempt that failed as a reason to try something else to give a longer life to the lightbulb.

Napoleon Hill told the famous story of R. U. Darby, who quit when he was three feet from gold. Darby got frustrated and sold his equipment to a junk man. With the help of an engineer, the new owner found gold three feet from where Darby had quit. Quitting cost Darby millions of dollars, but it taught him never to give up, and he became successful as an insurance salesman.

Richard M. DeVos, the cofounder of Amway and owner of the NBA basketball team Orlando Magic, once remarked, "If I had to select one quality, one personal characteristic that I regard as being most highly correlated with success, whatever the field, I would pick the trait of persistence. Determination. The will to endure to the end, to get knocked down seventy times and get up off the floor saying, 'Here comes number seventy-one!'"

Just remember that very few people succeed on their first attempt at anything worthwhile.

Each attempt is a risk, and every one can fail, but each attempt that is not successful should be seen as a step in the direction of the desired goal. Albert Einstein is usually thought of as one of the smartest men who ever lived, but a statement of his is very interesting; he once remarked, "It's not that I'm so smart, it's just that I stay with problems longer."

It is a mistake to assume that people succeed through success; much more often they succeed through failure. The experiences from which people gain the most value are failures. Successful people let failures teach them better self-management and self-control, so that they can avoid making the same errors in the future. There is a good chance that if you question a successful person, he will tell you that he learned the secret of success through trial and error, being thwarted, being challenged, and even being ridiculed by those proclaiming, "It can't be done."

Getting help from others, study, and reflection can all be helpful, but not to the degree that failure is a teacher. Failure can teach people discipline; it can teach them what to do and, probably more important, what not to do.

Many successful people make up their minds that they will persist, even if the failures continue, until they succeed. With the proper amount of persistence, their failures will only increase their resolve to succeed. A failure in one field of endeavor often points the way to another direction in which the person finds great success. Maybe the failure indicated other areas to which the person was better suited. It is impossible to calculate the number of the world's geniuses who have succeeded because of their earlier failures in life.

In many instances, failures are the only lessons needed to convince a person to take responsibility and use the knowledge she has acquired in order to succeed on the very next application of her skills and efforts. Just as steel is tempered by heat and made malleable so that it can be shaped into useful objects, the same is true of many successful people. Many people have been tempered in the furnace of trials and troubles, and only then, through failures in earlier attempts, have they finally achieved success and been rewarded for their efforts.

Giving up because of one, two, or even more failures is a very serious mistake. In war, the best generals are those who suffer defeat, but then reorganize and are ultimately victorious. Life is like a war in that there are many battles to be fought, but the true winner, even while still suffering from recent failures, lays plans and applies the necessary efforts to obtain the desired victory.

We must not allow biased views to prevail over what we know of people and events. Having our initial plans fail does not mean that the world is about to end or the destruction of life as it exists. Present failures, if they serve you, should teach you to be both wary and more persistent in the future so that you can obtain a deserving outcome for your efforts.

You must not let yourself fall into apathy and despair. You cannot afford to give up just because you have not yet succeeded. Take some time to reflect upon the thousands of attempts Thomas Edison made before developing the lightbulb he sought.

Read and study the life of Helen Keller. Though Helen Keller was blind and deaf from childhood, she overcame great disadvantages through sign language and writing. She wrote, "Character cannot be developed in ease and quiet. Only through experience of trial and suffering can the soul be strengthened, ambition inspired, and success achieved."

Read the life of Booker T. Washington or some other great American. It will inspire you to reach the success you seek. Born a slave, Booker T. Washington became one of the most successful Americans of his time—the late nineteenth and early twentieth centuries—and a statement that he made is still true today: "I have learned that success is to be measured not so much by the position that one has reached in life as by the obstacles which he has overcome while trying to succeed. . . . Out of the hard and unusual struggle through which he is compelled to pass, he gets a strength, a confidence, that one misses whose pathway is comparatively smooth by reason of birth and race."

How you view a failure will make all the difference in the world. Failure is the end only if you view it as such; you can instead view it as a lesson that you need to change your plans and put the new plans in action to obtain the desired results.

The idea that there is anyone who has never failed is a myth. All success is a trail of efforts that, when viewed up close, are seen to be more or less failures.

Often these efforts are not visible to others, but each individual failure is painfully obvious to the person who had cherished that plan, only to see it end in failure. When you have failed once, twice, or many times, discouragement can cause you to stop trying, but just remember that failure is the past experience of every successful person.

The most successful person is often the person with the most failures. Babe Ruth held the world record for the most home runs for many years, but he also held the record for the most strikeouts. This simply means that human nature allows us to remember the successes and give little, if any, thought to failures, but failures are a necessary part of the journey to success.

There is an interesting story about Babe Ruth: when he was asked what he thought about after striking out, Ruth said he thought about the next pitcher he was going to face because he knew that he was closer to his next home run. We should approach our failures in the same manner.

People who are failures usually go no farther than their first failure; they lag behind, expend little effort, and then subside into a life of discontent. By giving up, these people simply allow more room for those who refuse to quit. The statement that there is always room at the top is made more accurate by those poor souls who do not understand the success principles. It would be difficult to find a successful person whose success was not made possible by failures and who found that in retrospect, his failures were a blessing. Success is the result of perseverance, determined efforts, and, most of all, failures; however, successful people see their failures not as stumbling blocks, but as stepping-stones.

If success came without efforts, where would be the great success of the future?

It is the brave resolution to do better the next time that lays the groundwork for all real greatness. Many a great reputation has been destroyed by early success. Often success is harder to handle responsibly than failure is. People who achieve success in life too early can allow themselves to quit trying and rely too much on their past achievements. They overlook the fact that it is labor alone that renders any success certain, and that it is by the use of labor and energy that failure awakens one to the need to achieve. In many instances, however, the awakening comes too late!

Going the extra mile will separate you from the 95 percent of people who never reach their potential.

This is one of the simplest of success principles, yet it is the one that most people do not practice. The extra mile principle does not mean that you have to apply twice as much effort to truly succeed. Let me give you an easy example of what I mean.

In Major League Baseball, a lot of players have long-term contracts that total millions of dollars. Alex Rodriguez has a contract that totals $252 million. A ballplayer who comes to bat 10 times and gets 2 hits has a batting average of .200, and unless he improves, he will, before long, no longer be a major leaguer. But if that same player, by developing his skills and training, approaches the plate 10 times and gets 3 hits, he will increase his average to .300. A .300 hitter in the major leagues can write his own ticket. Just think: in the first example, he got 2 hits in each 10 times at bat and did not succeed, but when he improved and got 3 hits in 10 times, at bat, he embarked on an excellent career.

What changed was only 1 more hit in each 10 times at bat. He improved 10 percent, and that 10 percent improvement will make all the difference in a lifetime in the major leagues.

The same principle can be used in life. Over a period of time, if you improve only a little, the cumulative effect will pay huge rewards. Why would anyone not do a little extra to gain great rewards? Author and speaker Jim Rohn says that the reason can be attributed to the mystery of the mind. We cannot compel others to always go the extra mile, but there is no reason that each of us cannot apply the going the extra mile principle in our daily life, both in our business and in our personal life. The rewards may not be immediate, but the principle works every time.

You simply cannot reap what you have not sown. Going the extra mile entitles you to an increasing return. Try it; you will never regret your action.

While I was attending Clinch Valley College (now the University of Virginia-Wise), I took Betty Gilliam's art history class, which I enjoyed immensely. I learned to appreciate art, but I did not become an expert, although I may have thought I did. I had some early success at locating an oil painting, making pictures of it, and submitting them to Sotheby's (one of the largest auction houses in the world). Sotheby's made arrangements to pick up my painting, pack it for shipping, and take possession of it. Sotheby's put a picture of the painting in its catalog, which went to art collectors around the world. The painting was a success, and I felt like, "This is easy."

I was also collecting Russian art, and I consigned quite a few pieces, to an auction house in the Washington, DC, area. It seemed quite simple: just ship the paintings, have them insured, let the auction house sell my art, and then get a big check. Because I had been successful before I was knowledgeable, to say the least. However, I made one big error: I did not specify a minimum price, and much of the art was sold for less than my purchase price. After costs such as commissions, I lost money. Was this a failure? The answer is no because I learned a very valuable lesson, which was that one cannot assume that one will receive a profitable selling price. I did not need the money, but I was enjoying the art business. In future sales, I would specify a minimum selling price to prevent the same thing from happening again.

If this happened to most people, they would quit because they had failed. I did not fail, but I learned a lesson that would be of future benefit when I continued to purchase and sell art and other collectibles.

You cannot always be correct, but you can always use temporary failure to educate yourself.

The degree to which you learn to handle adversity will determine the extent to which you will know success. Whether you work for others or for yourself (your view should be that you are self-employed), each time you overcome adversity, the accomplishment will add to your self-worth. Your value in the workplace will improve each time you face adversity and solve a problem.

When an effort does not produce the results you wanted, you can accept it either as a failure or as a lesson. The view you take is of the utmost importance, and it will determine to a great extent whether you enjoy success.

Taking on adversity as a lesson will help make you a success in the future. Once you are successful, you will find that you will not need to make excuses. Success requires no explanation, but once a person accepts failure, her life is likely to be full of excuses, alibis, and blame toward others for her lot in life.

From experience, I can tell you that a lot more is learned from efforts that initially fail than from efforts that succeed.

4

PURPOSE AND BELIEF

If thou canst believe, all things are possible to him
that believeth.

— MARK 9:23

WHEN YOU HAVE selected your major purpose in life and made plans to reach your goal, you will be less likely to quit if a plan that you previously made fails.

Once you have developed your major purpose in life, the passion it creates will lead you to achieve greater self-discipline, self-reliance, and enthusiasm. Once you begin to work on your plans, you will see personal initiative begin to assist you and recognize that those who have a purpose, a plan, and personal initiative are the true success stories.

Purpose will help you develop a faith, and with that faith, confidence in yourself, and belief, you will succeed in your major purpose in life.

Vision helps us to see things as they can be, not as they are. The Old Testament says, "Without a vision the people perish." While it is important to study history, I think Thomas Jefferson's preference for the vision of the future rather than the history of the past reflects the fact that where we are going is much more important than where we have been.

Visualization is "seeing" a positive result and taking action to make that vision become a reality.

Develop a belief such that when you look into the mirror, you can say to yourself, "If it is to be, it is up to me." Once you believe in yourself, you will take the necessary steps to continue in the right direction and persist until you reach your goal.

In *Grow Rich! With Peace of Mind*, Napoleon Hill said, "When you speak of failure, you attract failure. When you speak of success, you attract success."

Napoleon Hill was telling the reader that the people who failed were those who kept on living with their failure. These people lived in the past tense, reliving the pain of what had happened to them in the past.

Those who succeeded spoke in the future tense. Their concentrated attention was on the future. They put failure in the past tense and directed their effort toward the future.

I have noticed in my career that people who are successful tend to speak well of other successful people. Failures or those who are on their way to failure often speak of those who are successful with either envy or malice.

When I worked in banking, often a customer would approach me after he had already been to another banking institution. The customer would tell me all the favorable terms he had been quoted. I would listen and then tell him what terms I could offer without saying anything bad about my competitors. Instead, I promised personal prompt attention and assured the customer that the bank was locally owned, with decisions being made locally and loans being kept locally for servicing. In other words, I talked positively about my employer without being negative toward the other banks.

The power to choose is a tremendous tool that is available to each of us. Choosing means making a decision. Even if we do nothing, we have made a choice. At the end of our lives, the station we have occupied is the result of the choices we have made. If we have made mostly better choices, we can expect better results.

Napoleon Hill, in his famous books such as *Succeed and Grow Rich Through Persuasion*, likened our choices to being given, at birth, two sealed envelopes, each of which contained the orders by which our lives were to be governed. One envelope would contain a long list of blessings that the individual would receive if she took possession of her own mind and used it to make the right choices. The other envelope would contain a long list of consequences that the person would receive if she did not use her power to make the correct choices.

Just recently I visited my 89-year-old mother after receiving a call telling me that one of my brothers had come to visit her while I was at the Napoleon Hill World Learning Center. While I was at Mom's, she wanted to know what I thought about her getting a new car. I told her that if she wanted one, that was fine—just to be sure that she got the value from it. My younger brother asked, "How long will you be driving? The car you have will probably last." My mother replied,

"My driver's license is good until I am 92." A positive belief is very important, not only to the length of our life, but also to its quality.

Every individual has the power to change his status in life by changing the nature of his beliefs.

The word *belief* is not to be confused with the word *wish*. The two words are not the same. Wishing for something will not bring it into being. Faith in one's goals is the way to take a wish, progress to a belief, and then with action move the belief into reality.

Faith in one's ability to accomplish a stated goal is the beginning of all achievement. If Edison had had only a wish and not faith in his belief that electricity could be tamed and a bulb could be created, the incandescent lamp, better known as the lightbulb, would not exist today. More than 10,000 attempts provided him with information concerning what did not work. Edison finally discovered the right material that would not only light up a room or a town, but would last a reasonable amount of time. He made the discovery because he believed he would succeed.

The state of mind known as faith opens us up to other sources of power and information that we would not be likely to find if we did not have faith in what we are trying to accomplish. We are not likely to seek help from others if we do not have faith in what we are trying to accomplish.

Be definite in everything you do, and never leave unfinished thoughts in your mind. Form the habit of reaching definite decisions on all subjects.

Everyone is born with the potential capacity to know what she wants and the ability to get it. Each person is born with the power to choose to exercise her prerogative to demand what she wants of life or neglect to do so.

Why do some people succeed and others fail, even though they live in the greatest nation on earth? Many people succeed with what may seem like surprising ease. Often those who fail had a better start than those who succeed. What happened? It is apparent that those who succeed had a belief system that told them that if they did certain things, they would be successful. Those who are not successful never believed that they would succeed. Failures make excuses such as not knowing the right people, lack of education, or bad luck, or just blame their failure on everybody but themselves.

If we do not develop a belief in ourselves, we are left to go through life without accomplishing worthwhile achievements.

Belief is the powerful force that will allow you to accomplish your goals. You need a belief in yourself if you are to get positive results.

Those with strong beliefs will often be laughed at, mocked, or even persecuted for their beliefs, especially when those beliefs are radical for their times. An excellent example would be the discovery of radio waves by Marconi. Guglielmo Marconi was born in Italy in 1874.

In 1894 while attending a private school, Marconi read an article that suggested the possibility of sending radio waves without wires (the invention of the radio).

Napoleon Hill wrote of Marconi's dream of a system of harnessing ether in *Think and Grow Rich*. Marconi's friend took him to a mental institution due to his belief of being able to send messages through the air.

He began studying wireless communication and in 1896 took out a patent and by 1901 Marconi was able to transmit signals across the Atlantic Ocean.

Marconi won the Nobel Prize in 1909 in physics for his work.

The reason for opposition to different beliefs is that people usually believe only what they want to believe and reject those beliefs that run counter to their own. It seems that many people are just not comfortable with changes. It has been said that people oppose those things that they do not understand and will not take the time or effort to learn.

Our beliefs about money and wealth are very important. In the New Testament of the Bible, more than half of the 24 parables are related to money. Money is mentioned far more often than prayer, and money is written about more than heaven and hell combined.

How important are our beliefs? Over the course of our lives, our beliefs will be what determine whether we are winners or losers. They will determine whether we are a part of humanity's solutions or a part of the problems. They will also determine whether we leave a legacy or whether we leave a life that was uneventful.

A person who has worthwhile accomplishments is someone who has beliefs to the degree that he has mental images of what he desires for the future.

It was Einstein who said that imagination was more important than knowledge. With a belief system, you can see images of what can occur in the future. These images will help you to believe in the future, develop plans, and have the persistence to see that those plans become reality.

Events that we are able to bring about happen because the beliefs we develop are so strong that we can hold on to them until our plans and actions can bring them to fruition.

Unless you have strong beliefs in what you want to become and develop those beliefs, it is highly unlikely that you will develop the plans and carry out the action needed to make you a highly successful person.

Belief is a force that will cause you to act; it can be said that belief motivates you to do what needs to be done to reach goals that you have previously set for yourself.

Wise men of the past realized and spoke of the fact that we are the result of our past thoughts. It is said that the overwhelming majority of people go to their graves without realizing the truth of this simple statement. If a person does not understand the importance of her thought process, then she is not likely to benefit from the proper use of her mind. The thought process has no limitations except those that we place on it. "You are today where your thoughts have brought you; you will be tomorrow where your thoughts take you," wrote James Allen.

There is a saying in Buddhism, "All that we are is the result of what we have thought." The simple fact is that your mind and the thoughts that you act on are what make you the person you are—either successful or unsuccessful.

At an early age, before I was of school age, my late father was an underground coal miner, and he told my brothers and me about the plants that grew wild in the mountainous area of southwestern Virginia where we lived. One of the plants was called mayapple, and once it was dug up and left in the sun to dry, it would sell for a few cents per pound. My father told me about the root and showed me how to dig it correctly. I did this and sold the roots for a few dollars; thus, even as a young child, I developed a belief that there was a way to make money. It was the biggest three dollars I had ever seen because I knew I had earned the money.

> *This city with all its houses, palaces, steam engines, cathedrals and huge, immeasurable traffic and tumult, what is it but a Thought, but millions of Thoughts made into one— a huge immeasurable Spirit of a Thought, embodied in brick, in iron, smoke, dust, Palaces, Parliaments, coaches, docks and the rest of it! Not a brick was made but some man had to think of the making of that brick.*

The meaning of these words from the pen of British writer Thomas Carlyle is that everything starts from the mind. An idea is the beginning of it all. Every event, condition, and thing is first an idea in someone's mind.

Such great undertakings as the pyramids were built in an era when things like machinery were not available as they are today. But what the ancients had were their minds, in which they conceived tremendous projects so vividly that they were able to overcome obstacles that all but a few would believe to be insurmountable. The pyramids were built of huge stones, and the workers basically had nothing but their hands.

What the workers had was the power of the mind, which has no limit except that which one applies to oneself.

Humans have a creative mind and are capable of creating results that have not existed before. However, a thought must exist before the mind can work. Remember, in all instances, a thought exists before a thing.

It is worth repeating many times that ideas within the mind are limited only by those limits placed on the mind by the individual.

Our mental attitude determines our condition and every experience we have in life. We can do only that which we think we can do. What we do, what we are, and what we have all depend upon what we think.

It is a fact that we can never express anything that we do not first have in our minds. If there is a secret, this is it—all power, all riches, and all success must first be thoughts built into our own minds.

I remember that when I was a young person, several weeks before Christmas, I was not thinking about toys or clothes that I might receive as gifts. I was thinking of ways to make money. I would think of holly, Christmas trees, and mistletoe that could be found in the woods and brought to the highway to sell to people who were traveling at this time of year. The thought of making money was so strong and I pictured it so vividly that its fruition seemed assured, as if it had already happened.

William James, the famous Harvard professor and psychologist, said that the greatest discovery of his generation was the discovery of the power of the subconscious mind. It's my belief that this was not only the greatest discovery of his generation but the greatest discovery of all time. What this means is that once this fact was known, people realized that they had within themselves the ability to control their surroundings. People are thereby separated from animals in that they are not at the mercy of luck or chance. With this discovery, people can engineer their own destiny.

A famous little book that I read many years ago and continue to read today on a frequent basis because of its powerful message is *As a Man Thinketh* by James Allen. Mr. Allen instructed us to "Dream lofty dreams, and as you dream, so shall you become. Your Vision is the promise of what you shall one day be; your Ideal is the prophecy of what you shall at least unveil."

The reason belief is important is that doubt that you can accomplish those things that would give you success will cause you to fail to take the steps that are needed if you are to succeed. All the literature available on success will not produce a successful person if belief is not present.

As humans, we tend to move where our thoughts take us. The problem lies in the fact that thoughts of failure, poverty, and the like will take us to those conditions.

Don't be afraid to commit. Commitments can either make you or break you. Commitments tell you who you are becoming. What we desire to be is what we commit to.

You either commit or you become like a tumbleweed, simply going in the direction of the wind.

Having the power to choose means that each of us decides to define himself either as a victim or as a survivor. Choosing to see yourself as a survivor gives you the power within your own mind to change your circumstances for the better.

Make a choice and develop a habit, and while choices make our habits, our habits then make us. Make good choices and you can expect good results; make bad choices and you can expect bad results.

As Napoleon Hill wrote, "Faith is a state of mind that may be described as an intensified form of self-reliance."

Faith in yourself is a necessary giant leap if you expect to travel the success journey. Belief is a component that is an absolute necessity if maximum positive results are to be obtained. The statement, "I will believe it when I see it," should be, "I will see it when I believe it."

Faith is essential if you are to become successful. The best definition of faith is probably that found in the New Testament, where Hebrews 11:1 states, "Faith is the substance of things hoped for, the evidence of things not seen." Things that you desire can become reality as, with your faith, you begin to see or visualize your desires becoming real.

Faith is to believe to be true that which has not yet materialized. Visualization of your objective and faith that you can realize it will prompt you to make plans and take the necessary action to bring your goals to reality.

Faith in yourself is necessary if you are to be a successful person. Things or plans that we seek to accomplish require faith that we can and will do those things that we desire.

Remember that people will believe in you only as much as you believe in yourself.

Belief is a state of mind that is essential for maximum results. You may say that belief is faith that you will reach a positive outcome that can be used to achieve success. Belief is faith that should be active or applied in your everyday plans.

You should relate to your belief system or faith as a source of energy, but if there is a secret, it is this: action is a key component. Having your mind under your complete control will allow you to remove limitations that you have previously applied to yourself or allowed others to apply to you.

Belief in yourself is a quality that you can develop. It does not mean having an ego that tells you that anything is possible with little or no effort.

Belief must be developed by removing all negative thoughts of poverty, illness, and lack, and selecting a goal that you are passionate about. Having a definite goal or purpose is where all of your future successes will start.

Making your working plans, altering them when necessary, getting the cooperation of others when needed, and persisting without quitting will help to give you a belief system that will reward you throughout your life. Remember that with desire, plans, and the assistance of others, action is the key. Remember the little quote, "Faith without action is dead."

You will discover that your belief system is needed if you are to turn desire into reality. Your belief system starts with the suggestions that you make to your subconscious mind. A belief is a part of you, giving you the realization that you have within you the ability to achieve what you think you can achieve as long as you desire to do so.

First and foremost, once you have the faith to achieve, you will acquire the necessary strength to bring about the goal you have in mind. You will begin to notice things, ideas, and people that can assist you. Belief in yourself will put you in touch with opportunities that you were not conscious of before you developed this belief.

Each accomplishment will add to this belief in yourself, and you will be truly in the small minority that uses belief in a positive manner to reach heights that others only dream of.

5

BOOKS

The man who doesn't read good books has no
advantage over the man who can't read them.

—MARK TWAIN 1835–1910

B OOKS CAN OPEN the door and show you a world of new ideas. In
many cases, books can also change your thoughts and your outlook on life. Books contain countless stories of young people who
overcame adversities and reached the top—examples that you can
relate to that will no doubt thrill you and inspire you to learn from
others, obtain the best education possible, and make something
worthwhile of yourself.

As you read inspirational stories, self-help books, biographies, and
autobiographies, you will probably hear a voice within you telling you
that you, too, can succeed. By reading about the success of others and
applying visualization, you can see the possibilities to become great,

just as others became great, that are present in your own life—even if it appeared that those others had very little opportunity to succeed.

A book can awaken the genius that lies within and allows someone to do wonderful things, even though at the beginning of that person's life, it appeared that he was not destined to do great deeds.

Books can not only awaken you to a knowledge of your possibilities but create what Dr. Napoleon Hill and other writers have called a *burning desire* to accomplish the type of great deeds that most people will only dream about. Books can arouse you and others to express the best that is within them rather than being content with lesser accomplishments.

In William M. Thayer's popular book *From Log-Cabin to the White House: Life of James A. Garfield,* written in 1881, the reader was told that the lives of great men are an inspiration to the young. These great men have within themselves perseverance, honesty, and other virtues necessary for success. The qualities of successful men are simple truths that successful men have demonstrated by their deeds.

What better way could there be for the inquiring young mind to learn success than studying men and women who became successful by the choices that they made and the actions that they performed?

Ralph Waldo Emerson wrote, "There is properly no history; only biography." If Emerson's statement is true, reading and learning from those who have succeeded is a profitable adventure. Learning about successful men and women from business, art, medicine, education, or other fields that benefit humanity will excite the reader to become successful as well.

The real reason to read about successful men and women is to learn how they achieved their success. These biographies are all true lessons in life from which the reader can glean life-changing ideas and examples.

BOOKS

Poly I. Emenike grew up in poverty in Nigeria—not the ideal background for success.

Poly read Dr. Napoleon Hill's books and gives credit to them for his success. Having earned a PhD after receiving a master's degree in economics, Poly is chairman and CEO of Neros Pharmaceutical Company and an outstanding humanitarian and philanthropist. The Neros Soccer Complex in Nigeria is the result of his contributions. As a result of reading Dr. Hill's books, Dr. Poly has donated more than a quarter of a million dollars to the nonprofit Napoleon Hill Foundation. This shows you the power of books and the path to success.

However, books do not give us only stories or examples that tell us what to do. As in the Bible (or in classics such as *Aesop's Fables*), the reader can find two completely different types of stories. You should absorb not only those stories that are used as positive examples, but also those stories that are used as negative examples or warnings. Basically, one type of story tells us to do as these people did; the other type tells us *not* to do as these people did.

Before you leave a legacy, be sure that the stories you leave behind are stories of examples and not warnings.

A title of a book can help bring attention to that book. Surely that was the case with Napoleon Hill's bestselling classic *Think and Grow Rich!* This book still sells hundreds of thousands of copies worldwide each year. As great as this title is, *Think and Grow Rich!* would have succeeded under almost any title—for it is not just what's printed on the cover but what is inside that makes a book a success or a failure. Nonetheless, I cannot imagine any potential reader who would not be intrigued by the promise inherent in Hill's title. I think also of such contemporary books as *The Secret* and *Seven Habits of Highly Effective People* as examples of books that pique people's interest by their titles alone.

All good books on self-help or success should have stories that flame the imagination of the readers. The overwhelming majority of these books will relate the histories of individual men and women who began in less than favorable circumstances, yet succeeded in various fields of human endeavor. All stories of successful men and women show that these people exercised indomitable will, concentrated on worthwhile goals, and were persistent as they moved from the humblest ranks to positions of great service and recognition. These true stories show how men and women, sometimes starting in poverty, often struggled in the face of failures that would give most people a reason—or excuse—to become discouraged and quit.

Stories of people going from failure to success serve as examples of what can happen and the results of a continuous forward march.

In February 2004, I was in Palm Springs, California, and heard the late entertainer Art Linkletter speak about the progress that had occurred in his lifetime. Linkletter was born in 1912, when the life expectancy of a male living in the United States was about 47 years (today it is about 78 years). Extending the life expectancy came about in the twentieth century. This tremendous progress was made possible by men and women who developed their hidden powers for the betterment of humanity. Art Linkletter himself was the perfect example. He lived to be almost 100, and he was inspiring and productive until the end.

Linkletter will be forever remembered for his great bestseller, *Kids Say the Darnedest Things*, which became part of Americans' everyday language.

My late friend Charlie "Tremendous" Jones, a noted author, world-class speaker, and owner of Executive Books, was a lover, collector, and seller of books. Charlie was so influenced by books that he gave away thousands and thousands of them. When he came across what he considered to be a book with a valuable message, he was likely to send his friends not just a free copy of the book, but a case or more for distribution so that others might benefit from the message.

Charlie also proved his love for books by donating to Lancaster Bible College in Lancaster, Pennsylvania, where the library is named in his honor. (If you call Executive Books at 1-800-233-2665, and you are lucky enough to be placed on hold, you will hear a delightful tune about books while you are waiting.)

Someone once said that leaders are readers, and when he said that, he sent a powerful message. As proof of that message, Charlie Jones's *Life Is Tremendous* has sold more than two million copies and is a must-read in the personal development field.

Before I became executive director of the Napoleon Hill Foundation, I was a trustee of the foundation and the late W. Clement

Stone was chairman of the board. I made a point of sitting next to Mr. Stone at board meetings and other events, such as the ground-breaking for the Napoleon Hill World Learning Center at Purdue University Calumet in Hammond, Indiana. The Napoleon Hill Foundation has been one of the school's largest contributors. The World Learning Center houses the precious archives of Dr. Hill. From the center, Director Judith Williamson oversees the educational component of the Napoleon Hill Foundation, which includes classes, seminars, Internet courses, and extensive education in prisons.

W. Clement Stone's own background provided few clues that one day he would become so wealthy that he could give away several hundred million dollars to charitable causes before he died at the age of 100.

Stone grew up on the Chicago's rough South Side with his mother, who became a widow before Stone began school. At age 6, Stone was out on the streets of Chicago selling newspapers to contribute to the household income. By the age of 13, he owned his own newsstand. Stone's life shows the lessons he learned from experience and books while he was growing up.

Clement Stone was a great reader and collector of books. As a youth, he read the tremendously successful Horatio Alger books—he read more than 50 of the success books and later had several hundred copies of the books in his library, which he gave to the Napoleon Hill Foundation along with thousands of other books from his collection. This valuable collection is housed at the Napoleon Hill World Learning Center.

Stone read *Think and Grow Rich!* by Napoleon Hill when it was published in 1937. He gave his employees the book, and his insurance firm grew from a $100 investment to a billion-dollar business. Stone spent more than 60 years praising *Think and Grow Rich!* and its positive effect. He even used as his company's stock symbol the letters PMA, for positive mental attitude, one of the principles of success.

I collected Horatio Alger books and read the stories—stories of young boys who became successful and stories of human qualities that teach persistence, honesty, and hard work. Not only did I discover that Stone read and collected books like Horatio Alger's, but also that James Oleson, a friend of Stone's and the president of the Napoleon Hill Foundation, also read and collected Horatio Alger books. Successful people are readers, and readers are leaders.

If you are not familiar with Bernard Baruch, it would be a good idea for you to read his autobiography, *My Own Story*. In the preface, Baruch tells of having known seven U.S. presidents, from Woodrow Wilson to Dwight D. Eisenhower. This autobiography was written when Baruch was 87. As a young boy, when he saw others' accomplishments, he was driven to try to do the same thing himself.

Baruch tells the reader that he found that failings and mistakes were a far better teacher than success.

I cannot overstress the importance of reading good books such as biographies, autobiographies, self-help books, and varied other books to broaden your education.

Below is an article written by Judith Williamson on reading which appeared in Issue 109 of Napoleon Hill's ezine on February 20, 2009. The ezine is published on a weekly basis by the Napoleon Hill World Learning Center at Purdue University Calumet. To sign up for your free weekly subscription of the ezine please visit www. naphill.org.

Dear Readers,

If you do nothing else but read to a child, you are providing a great service. It's been said that "Readers are Leaders," and in order to grow a leader you must engender in youth a love for reading. By my own admission, I am a "bookaholic." And, I will tell you a little secret. Don Green, the executive director for the Foundation is too. We both simply love books and reading. Don brags that he has several books on his nightstand that he reads simultaneously. My husband states that I have a good portion of the Library of Congress in our home. I favor self-help literature because of the work that I do, but my overall interest in books is varied. I believe that my mother brought my awareness to reading and what books could do for a person well before I could read by myself.

In an email that I recently received from Dr. J. B. Hill, Napoleon Hill's grandson, he enlightened me regarding some educational issues he uncovered while doing genealogy work on the Hill family. Dr. J. B. Hill states:

Women have always been the source of essential education in the Hill family. My Irish mother taught me to read; my grandmother taught my dad to read before he was 5, my step great grandmother civilized and educated Napoleon, and my GG grandmother probably educated Napoleon's father. Last week, I watched my bride Nancy teaching our daughter to read and realized that it will be the same in this generation. I have the role of protector, provider, disciplinarian, ethics instructor, and Daddy—but Nancy is the real teacher to my children.

In response, I replied:

Sounds like you have really traced the Hill family history and uncovered trends that will benefit future generations. My mother too taught me to read. I was lazy in first grade because my mother read to me so much and I enjoyed it. It was a favorite pass time of mine. However, when the first grade teacher threatened to hold me back because I couldn't read, my mother countered with saying: "What do you mean, she can't read? We read all the time!" When I got home after that memorable parent-teacher conference, my mother chastised me for not reading and intuitively knew what to do. She said, "From now on, I will read to you from your favorite storybooks, but only every other page. You must read a page after I read a page."

That's all it took to get me to be an active reader not a passive listener. Mom—whose birthday is Feb. 20—has been gone since 1990, but she is in my heart every day. She was smarter than all the teachers with the degrees and teaching experience. Like the women in the Hill family, my mother knew the secret to turning on the light of learning. And, it has made all the difference to each of us, right? Today, from a first grader who couldn't/wouldn't read, I hold a K-12 administrative license as a reading specialist among other degrees. Also, I know that the best teacher is the one nearest the pupil, not the one standing over the reluctant student trying to force feed education. Whether it's through a typewriter or a storybook, a smart teacher knows how to catch a child's desire to learn and put it into productive action. I wish families would recognize this, and use the magic inside their children to unleash their potential. Sounds like your wife is doing a great job with your two! Congratulations.

By sharing these two personal stories with you, I hope that you begin to understand the significance of reading in a person's life. Good books lead to good thoughts that create good lives. Don't waste the opportunity to be a reader. Where else can you have a one-on-one lesson with an expert? It is the best value on the planet. Pick up a book and read! I guarantee that you will learn a great deal. Moms cannot be wrong. And, Dr. J. B. Hill, Don Green and I give reading our strongest endorsement.

Be Your Very Best Always!
Judith Williamson, Director
Napoleon Hill World Learning Center

Lord Byron, in his classic book-length poem *Don Juan*, wrote, "A small drop of ink/ . . . makes thousands, perhaps millions, think."

Reading the right books should cause you to think, learn from others, be inspired to the point where you will select a worthy purpose in life, make plans, and take action to succeed.

Good books can help you plan your life. In a novel, the author writes the story and the ending. Reading a self-help book will allow the reader to prepare her life and to write her own ending.

Read the book as if the author is writing to you. Underline phrases that appeal to you. Make cards with information that matters to you, and place the cards where you can see them daily. Whether the cards are on your desk, in your pocket, or somewhere else, the fact that you review the messages often will reinforce them to your subconscious mind. Go back and read the material on a regular basis. You probably didn't learn your ABCs or multiplication tables in one attempt, and valuable information that will assist you on the road to success is no different.

I have learned that reading good books leads to a better future and a life of worthwhile purpose—and you can learn this same important lesson. When you plan for success, it will be absolutely necessary that you maintain a good reading program.

Reading should not be limited to books, but should include varied types of material. For example, if your career is in finance, banking, or investments, you will want to read constantly in order to stay current. Also read biographies of successful men and women, both past and present. You can learn from Carnegie, Rockefeller, and other giants of the past.

Today's financial leaders, such as Warren Buffett and Peter Lynch, will keep you informed on important matters that you need to know.

Just imagine doing the same job as others who do not have a good reading program. By having such a program, you will position yourself to be a leader instead of a follower in whatever job or organization you choose to work.

A good friend and mentor of mine, James A. Brown, Jr., known to his friends simply as Jim, once told me the following story:

> *I remember the seventh grade when I was encouraged to read books. It was the first time I had been tested as to what grade level I had reached—and guess what? Here I was in the seventh grade, and I tested at fifth-grade level. My teacher told the class she would make a record of the books*

we read by putting a star by each name every time we read a book and gave her a two-page report. By the end of the year, nobody in my class was even close to the number of books I had read.

I was, along with my sister, being raised on $125 per month by our mother, and knowing I faced poverty every day. I worked at anything, including fixing flats or whatever, to make money, and I developed a work ethic which is still with me today.

He also continued to read.

Jim went on to finish Grundy High School, located in the mountains of southwestern Virginia where poverty that endured from one generation to another was common. He then attended Virginia Tech in Blacksburg, where he obtained a degree in engineering. Jim began working at a coal company for $600 per month, but he had much bigger plans for his life. By age 29, he had started a coal company of his own and organized a bank. Among his accomplishments, in addition to mining coal and drilling for natural gas, he has bred and raised some of the finest Arabian horses in the world. Jim has also been successful in land development and manufacturing on a grand scale.

Jim Brown would fit almost anyone's definition of success—he's still married to his college sweetheart, Bliss, and they are the parents of a son and a daughter who have both been successful on their own. If success begins in the home, he is a perfect example.

I can only fathom what Jim's career might have looked like if that seventh-grade teacher had not encouraged him to read. Guess what: Jim still is an avid reader of good books today—books of every kind and category.

In 1995, singer songwriter and actress Dolly Parton was looking for a way to help the children of her native Sevier County, Tennessee, become better readers, learn to love books, and bring books to their homes. (Sevier is in eastern Tennessee, mountain country, just over the state line from where I am writing this.) Then, in 1996, Dolly Parton and her Dollywood Foundation launched the children's book program called Imagination Library.

Within only a few years, the program grew to the point where it is mailing millions of books to more than 40 U.S. states, Canada, and the United Kingdom.

Christy Crouse, the regional director of the Dollywood Foundation who operates the Imagination Library program, is a native of Wise County. She is responsible for the contact that led to the creation of the Imagination Library—first in Wise County, then spreading to the other counties in southwest Virginia.

Dolly Parton's connection to the southwestern part of Virginia would seem to be a natural. Both areas are mountainous with a high rate of school dropouts, which leads to a continuing cycle of poverty and low levels of self-esteem among much of the population.

Many people in southwestern Virginia have known Dolly ever since she appeared on a country music TV station that was seen in Wise County and the area surrounding it when she was a teenager. Today she is known the world over, not only as an entertainer of unparalleled talent, but as an educator and philanthropist who shares her hopes and dreams for others through books.

Ms. Parton writes and plays country music, which is a type of music enjoyed by most of the people in the mountains of eastern Tennessee, where she grew up, and in southwestern Virginia.

Dollywood, the theme park she founded at the entrance to the Great Smoky Mountains, is a favorite vacation spot for the people living in southwestern Virginia. But her vision and generosity are felt far from our familiar mountain "hollers."

6

DESIRE AND DISCIPLINE

The true worth of a man is to be measured by the objects he pursues.

—MARCUS AURELIUS

NAPOLEON HILL SAID, "If you would achieve great success, plant in your mind a strong motive!" You will find it easier to be successful if you first know what you want. After that, you must make plans and take action. You probably will not know all the answers before you begin, but you must not let that prevent you from starting on your road to success.

When you discover the powers of your mind, you are beginning to move toward whatever you most desire from life. Remember that life is not static, and that each of us is either moving in the direction of his goals or moving away from them.

Elbert Hubbard once said, "Tell me what you desire most in life and I will tell you who can do the most to help you get it." When Hubbard was asked who that person was, he said, "Look in the mirror, and you will see him."

I have read more than 1,000 books that deal with success, some of which would be classified as self-help, others as inspirational, and still others as biographies of successful people. All success stories start when a person wants to improve her position in life and that desire is intense enough to cause her to take action to change her circumstances. You might think that everyone would want to improve her position in life, but if the wish is just a wish, it amounts to no more than a dream. Only when the desire has become so strong that it is what writers have called a burning desire or passion will the person take action to change her lot in life.

To begin your journey, you must begin with the right ideas that can grow the desire until it becomes a burning desire.

DESIRE

Napoleon Hill has defined a burning desire as the starting point of all achievement.

Shane Morand had more than just a desire or hope to have his own company. He had a burning desire to create a worldwide sales organization.

In 2008, Shane Morand, Bernie Chua, and others founded Organo Gold. Today, Bernie Chua is Organo's CEO, Shane Morand is cofounder and global master distributor, and Holton Buggs is VP of sales, and together they operate one of the fastest-growing direct sales companies in the world.

Organo Gold has hundreds of thousands of distributors and estimates that it will have a million by 2015 selling coffee, the number two commodity in the world (behind oil). Shane Morand's desire started in 2008 when he sold his first box of Organo Gold coffee, which contains a Chinese mushroom called Ganoderma that is known for its health benefits.

Find your desire and pursue it as if your success depends on it—and it really does.

There are both great destinies and obstacles in your future, but you were born with the powers and capabilities that will let you improve your situation and be a success. You have the gifts that will let you make the right choices and take action, with your success or failure hanging in the balance.

Robert Collier penned a wonderful seven-volume set of little books in 1926 called *The Secret of the Ages.* In one volume, Collier wrote a section on desire, and he asked the question, "If *you* had a fairy-wishing ring, what one thing would you wish for? Wealth? Honor? Fame? Love? What one thing do you desire above everything else in life?"

The power to become what you want to be, to get what you crave, and to accomplish what you strive for lies within you. You are the one person who can bring it from within and go toward the accomplishment you so want.

You can be whatever you make up your mind to be. If you are unhappy, poor, or unsuccessful, the fault lies within you. Your potential has no limits, but you must realize this and have a strong belief in it, one that is strong enough to get you to put plans in motion.

I am the executive director of the Napoleon Hill Foundation and responsible for a worldwide organization that is a multimillion-dollar business. If you visited me in my office, you would see a sign that reads, "If it is to be, it is up to me." As long as you fail to take responsibility for your future, but instead rely on government hand-outs or the support of friends and relatives, then you will not know success.

Within you lie the abilities to overcome obstacles. As sure as night and day, success will come your way if you follow the success principles and persist.

Without self-discipline, you have no reason to expect to be successful.

The key to achieving what you want out of life lies in establishing meaningful goals. You must continue to feed your minds with thoughts and ideas that are consistent with your goals. Next, you must take action and persist. The one thing we know for certain is that the system works.

I remember the first time I met W. Clement Stone in Chicago, Illinois. I had received an invitation to attend a board of trustees meeting of the Napoleon Hill Foundation at O'Hare Airport.

Prior to meeting Mr. Stone—and everybody I knew called him Mr. Stone, although it was said that when President Reagan called, he addressed him as Clem—I had read Mr. Stone's books.

At the time, Mr. Stone was chairman of the board of the Napoleon Hill Foundation. He was in his nineties. Always dressed as a successful businessman, Mr. Stone was an imposing figure.

I had read his book *The Success System That Never Fails*. This is a must-read for anyone who is interested in how to be successful. As mentioned earlier, Mr. Stone grew up on Chicago's tough South Side, lost his father when he was quite young, and was out on the street selling newspapers at the age of 6. He was often beaten by other boys, but he persisted and began to accept responsibility for his future at a very early age.

From being around Mr. Stone (which I considered a privilege), I learned that he spoke of decisions. Decisions were important, but once a decision was reached, then a proper course of action was fundamental to success. You would get the same advice from Stone's writings: action was critical if you were to travel the success journey.

Unless you accept responsibility for your success, you will never be successful.

If you fail to take the responsibility for your success, your conversations will be filled with talk of blame, failure, envy, and other negative terms that will take you farther down the road of failure.

You can have high goals, develop good plans, and have a pleasing personality and many other desirable qualities. But to be truly successful, you must have discipline. Without discipline, you will be among the majority who will look over their lives and think about "what could have been."

———————————————

Discipline is a quality that you must learn, and the quicker you learn discipline and put it to use, the faster you will travel on the journey that others who have little or no discipline will only dream of.

———————————————

7

GOALS

You have to find something that you love enough to take risks, jump over the hurdles and break through the brick walls that are always going to be placed in front of you. If you don't have that kind of feeling for what it is you are doing, you'll stop at the first giant hurdle.

— GEORGE LUCAS

ACROSS THE COMMONWEALTH of Virginia, historical markers honor important places in the state's history. Some of the markers are very significant in the history of the entire United States, a valuable resource that represents the history and culture of America. For example, some of the several hundred markers that have been erected within the state's boundaries identify the birthplace of President Woodrow Wilson, Robert E. Lee's boyhood home, the University of

Virginia, and President James Monroe's birthplace. Eight presidents of the United States were born in Virginia.

The state Department of Historic Resources is made up of historians, architects, archaeologists, and activists who are committed to providing education on historic sites.

In 1930, the first highway marker guidebook was published. The original intent of the marker program was to create interest throughout the country in Virginia's history and to promote tourism. Today the markers are a valuable source of information to those traveling on Virginia's highways.

The reason I tell this story is that in 1993, I had a goal of getting a state marker erected to honor Napoleon Hill, author of the classic book *Think and Grow Rich!*, which has been continuously in print since its publication and has sold millions of copies all over the world.

I did not achieve this goal within the time I had set to complete it.

I wrote the Virginia Historical Markers program, but the reply was not promising, to say the least. Instead of quitting, I started different plans. I contacted local and national political figures. I got a list of the members of the Virginia Historical Society and contacted them individually. One of the people I contacted was Robert Wrenn, who was the circuit court clerk, and he had read Napoleon Hill and been inspired by what he had read.

As I contacted others, the process gained momentum until I got approval from the Virginia Historical Society to place a Virginia historical marker on U.S. Highway 23 near Wise, Virginia. Highway 23 is the most traveled road in the area, so when the marker was erected, there was a large turnout of interested citizens.

**Often you will fail in your time element,
but remember that failing is not final
until you quit trying.**

When you take action on a goal, your plans often do not work out as projected. If you wait until you have completely perfect plans, you are likely to never get started. Once you have developed a burning desire, make plans and begin. If your plans need to change, or if the goal takes longer, you should still feel satisfied if you began what was a worthy goal for you.

It will take self-discipline, but if you do not have it, you have no reason to expect to have a successful life.

In 1990, at the University of Virginia-Wise, I was called upon to cochair a capital campaign to raise needed funds for the college. The economy in Virginia did not allow the state to provide the college with the funds it needed for scholarships, building projects, and operating a first-class liberal arts school.

Dr. Brent Kennedy was employed by the university as provost, and his job was to guide the campaign. Dr. Kennedy had a PhD in philanthropy from the University of Tennessee and had worked in fund-raising at Georgetown University and for the Jimmy Carter Presidential Library, among other places. I had known Kennedy and his family for many years, and I was confident of his ability to head a successful campaign. I met with him prior to the start of the campaign, and he convinced me that we could raise $20 million.

At our first meeting, we discussed various topics, such as who each of us knew who would be good prospects and what could be accomplished with the campaign. A suggestion that we try to raise $4 million was made, based on the fact that in the best year to date, gifts had amounted to $1 million. The campaign was to run for four years, and that goal appeared to be logical to some members of the group. I liked Dr. Kennedy's suggestion of $20 million, but we were told that should we fail miserably, it would be a terrible public relations fiasco. I still thought we could raise $20 million, but the group settled on a goal of $13 million.

During the four years, not only did we raise $13 million, but we surpassed the $20 million amount also!

The reason I tell you this story is to show you that most people set their goals too small and fail to develop a belief in themselves that enables them to set goals that may seem impossible at the time. Some of us saw the goal as $20 million and worked to see that what we envisioned would be brought about by the end of the campaign.

Most people do not set goals, for some unknown reason. Nearly everyone has dreams of a better life and of improving her health, wealth, and comforts. But surprisingly, the overwhelming majority of people do not write down what they want to accomplish.

Written goals can serve as a contract with yourself. The goals must be your own goals and not those of someone else, such as your parents or your spouse. The reason the goals need to be yours is that you are not likely to develop a burning desire to succeed unless the goals belong to you.

The goals should be measurable. After all, if you cannot measure your goals, how will you know that you have accomplished them?

Goals that you set out to accomplish also need a date or timeline. For example, if you have a personal goal of finishing your college degree, you must have a date by which you intend to complete it. If you do not commit to finishing your degree by, for example, December 31 of *this year*, you probably will not start taking courses, but instead will keep telling yourself that you are going to take courses you need someday. The problem with this is that *someday* is not on the calendar, and you have not committed yourself.

GOALS

In 1972, a young man from the United States was a member of the Olympic team in the decathlon. He placed third overall in the ten events, losing out to a Russian.

In his biography, Bruce Jenner told about reading *Think and Grow Rich!* and about setting goals for himself for the next Olympic Games, which were to be held in 1976. He set specific goals for each of the ten events that he was to participate in.

In 1976, Jenner won the gold medal in the Summer Olympics, setting a new world record in the decathlon. When he won the event, a spectator handed him an American flag, and he took a victory lap. This gesture has been repeated at the Olympic Games ever since.

Goals are important and should be written down with an assigned date for their completion.

Another point in goal setting is that if you do not reach your goal by the date you previously set because of some unforeseen circumstances such as a job loss, a job transfer, or health issues, taking longer than you anticipated does not mean that you have failed.

Again I would like the reader to reflect on the word millionaire because it is what you become during the process that matters most, not the fact that after following the success principles, you find out that you have a net worth of a million dollars or more. Still, as motivational speaker, author, and businessman Jim Rohn has said, "The word *millionaire* has a nice sound to it."

While becoming a millionaire will not do what it might have done 50 or 100 years ago, it still can be a great help in establishing your own legacy.

Dream big, set big goals, make plans, get started, get the help of others when needed, and follow Mark Twain's advice. Don't walk away from negative people but run. Negative people will tend to discourage you while you are chasing your goals.

Why should you have goals? There are many reasons. First, if you knew with the utmost assurance that you could set meaningful, worthwhile goals and would certainly succeed, would you set goals?

People who are goal-oriented are much more likely to be successful.

Having studied goal setting for years, I am often reminded of Michelangelo, who said, "The greatest danger for most of us is not that our aim is too high and we miss it, but that it is too low and we reach it."

When you are working on setting your goals, there are different ways you can set them, but some steps are mandatory. For example, to begin with, the goals must be your goals, not what someone else wants for you. A goal should be something for which you have a passion; otherwise, when an obstacle gets in your way, you are likely to quit. A goal will cause you to get up early, pursue it with a passion, look for other solutions when obstacles arise, seek the help of others, and do whatever it takes to reach your goal. Also, the goal you choose needs to be something that you can measure.

For example, should your goal be to lose weight, the amount you want to lose should be reasonable, and you should have a definite date by which you will reach your ideal weight. For example, if your goal is to drop 30 pounds, you cannot reasonably accomplish this in three days, but if you break down the goal to losing 30 pounds in three months, you would need to lose only 10 pounds a month, or about 5.3 ounces a day, which is very reasonable.

Here is the system that I have personally used for many years to set goals; it will work for you. Each year, toward year-end, I spend some quiet time with a legal pad and pen and write down what I would like to accomplish in the next year, three years, five years, and ten years. I may list many things, but studying them will allow me to determine which are the most important to me. Next, I list the goals on 3 × 5 index cards.

For more than 30 years, I have carried these cards in my inside coat pocket. Each day, and sometimes several times a day, I would take the cards out and review them. I would mentally ask myself what I was doing or planning to do that would move me closer to each goal.

Again, the first step is that the goal must be yours and yours alone. It must not be that of your parents, your spouse, or anyone but you. You must claim 100 percent ownership of your goals. Inspiration comes from within ourselves.

Second, the goal must be realistic. Being realistic does not mean that the goal cannot be big. Studying goals, I have discovered that most people set their goals too small, and that this also applies to me. It costs no more to set big goals than it does to set small ones. Being realistic, for example, means that if you are 60 years old, becoming an all pro in the NBA is not going to happen. Your desire to be in the professional basketball league is driven by your love for basketball. You can still be around basketball by becoming an employee of a team, a team owner, or an agent. Mark Cuban does not have the talent to be a professional basketball player, but he made hundreds of millions in the technology field, and then bought the NBA's Dallas Mavericks.

Next, the goal must have a date attached to it that is written down with the goal. This becomes a contract with yourself. You will need reminders of a time when you were your ideal weight or pictures of someone with what you consider an ideal physique to help motivate you. You must not see yourself as an overweight person, but you need to see yourself at your desired weight.

Goals should be things that require a great deal of effort and that you have a passion to accomplish. They should stretch your talents and imagination because we all do best when we are challenged. You will no doubt discover that goals that help the world become a better place will give you the most satisfaction.

Goal setting works, and if you think you don't have time to set goals, you are missing the key ingredient of success.

> *The last of the human freedoms [is] to choose one's*
> *attitude in any given set of circumstances.*
> — VIKTOR FRANKL

Here are some pointers that will help you develop goals:

✦ Goals are simply a list of the things you expect to accomplish.
✦ Goals must be written down so that they become a contract with yourself.

✦ Goals belong to you and are not things that your parents or others set for you. Ownership of goals must be 100 percent yours.

✦ Goals must have a date by which you will accomplish them; otherwise you will be living in a fairy tale of "someday": someday I will finish college, someday I will start an exercise program, and so on. *Someday* is not on the calendar and is a polite way of lying to ourselves about not getting started.

Plans to accomplish your goals may not work at first and may need to be adjusted. After all, we learn from experience, which is the greatest teacher.

Anything great that is to be accomplished will require the help of others. Work with those who can help you and who have expertise in the area that you lack.

Live your dream, and do not let others have a negative influence on you.

Remember that others have overcome obstacles that are most likely much more difficult than yours. Develop an attitude that says, "They did it, and I can too, and I will." Remember that everything begins with our thought process. Here is where we need to realize that "the imagination is the workshop of the mind, in which is fashioned every idea, plan and mental pictures." (Napoleon Hill's *Think and Grow Rich!* Ch. 6)

Don't be afraid to set big goals; it costs no more than setting small goals.

In discussing success at anything, attitude has to be taken into consideration. You could say that attitude is everything. But beyond having a good attitude, plans and determination are absolutely necessary.

Every self-help book you read will probably tell you that success is reaching goals that you have set for yourself.

The problem with defining success as reaching a certain goal, such as accumulating a certain sum of money, is that when you get there, it may not seem like success. When money is the goal, you will often pay too big a price for it. If acquiring money means that you will not be spending time with your family, will not be doing community service, or will be doing things that compromise your integrity, then, upon reflection, you will probably feel that this was not what you meant by being a success.

Nothing within the realm of possibility can deny success to the person who takes intelligent actions and is persistent.

Every person carries within him the key to either success or failure. It seems that everyone would desire success, but the problem lies in taking the necessary steps to be a winner.

The action that is necessary if you are to succeed is always preceded by a great purpose. Life is full of examples that show great human achievements that have been proportional to how great the purpose was and how much action was involved.

To be successful, you need to decide on a noble purpose and pursue it with all your might.

Nothing can assure failure as fast as uttering such words as, "My life is aimless."

A strong purpose or aim gives direction, will power, and the necessary energy to persevere in all one's efforts. Aim and self-discipline assures succes, and even with talent and intellect, a person with no purpose or aim in life will be a failure. We should have some definite purpose in front of us, some goal that we are striving to reach; we cannot expect to reach great heights without a worthy purpose in mind.

Nature holds for each of us everything that she needs to make her useful and happy, but nature requires people to labor for what they get. Overcoming the obstacles in front of each of us requires strong efforts and perseverance.

Every day, each of us should do something that moves him closer to a better life. Our lives must have a definite plan of action if we are to be a success in life.

Purposes require work, but it is vain indeed to expect results from purposes only. Every step should be a move toward the accomplishment of the purpose that we desire.

In order to reach her potential, each person should begin with a purpose, the best possible plan, efforts that use most of her talents, and association with others who have talents that complement her own.

8

HABITS AND PERSEVERANCE

Well begun is half done.

— ARISTOTLE

THE KEY TO achieving what we want out of life lies in establishing our goals and then continuing to feed our minds with thoughts and ideas that are consistent with our goals and taking action. The one thing you can be assured of if you follow these steps you will realize the system has worked for others and it will work for you.

When someone said that we make our habits, and then our habits make us, that person made a true statement. It's true whether the habit is a good one, like reading good books every day or regular exercise, or a bad one, like using tobacco. Our habits can have a tremendous effect on our lives, and whether that effect is negative or positive is a choice we each make.

The late J. Paul Getty, whom *Fortune* magazine once called "the richest man in the world," wrote *How to Be Rich*. In this book, Mr. Getty related a wonderful example of what habits can do for us or to us. Some habits are good, and some are bad. Our accumulation of choices determines whether the habits we acquire will benefit us or will be a detriment to our future.

Mr. Getty told about driving through France and stopping for the night in a small town during a bad rainstorm. He awoke during the night with a desire to smoke, but he found that he had only an empty pack. He started to put on his clothes to go out into the storm, but then he realized that the habit had him. He related that having discovered his problem, he returned to bed and dropped the cigarette habit.

The thing to remember about habits is that we make our habits and then our habits make us.

Habits formed from continued practice can have a tremendous effect on your success, either positive or negative. For example, if you are continually late, you are ignoring the fact that time is money, and the message you are sending to others is not favorable. The importance of being on time applies to appointments, returning phone calls, paying your debts, or returning books to the local library.

Being prompt sends a signal to others that you can be counted on and that you consider other people's time important. Just as being prompt sends a good message, being late gives the reason to tell others that you are lazy, are undependable, or simply do not care.

Our physical traits are pretty much received from our parents, but what we become we do ourselves through the use of our mental processes.

Physical traits are things such as hair color, eye color, size, and the like, many of which we have little or no control over.

The important qualities that each of us can control make up our social environment. These qualities are habits that each of us can change for the better or for the worse. You will discover that the earlier you form habits, the more likely it is that they will remain with you. Again, this applies to both good and bad habits.

It is common to view habits in a negative manner, suggesting that developing habits is always adverse, rather than viewing them in a manner that suggests that habits can be not only not adverse but helpful in developing qualities that will improve our lives.

As well as looking only at habits that are bad for you, such as excessive alcohol use or smoking, you need to look at habits that, once established, are good for you and will improve your self-worth and confidence.

Habits are simply a result of repeating things. Every mental act becomes easier each time it is repeated. The same results can be expected with each new undertaking to which you commit yourself.

Each new habit will get easier each time you take action. The more often you repeat a habit, the firmer it will be, and you will be less apt to stray from it. Also, remember that a habit such as using a treadmill for 30 minutes a day gets easier to repeat the more you perform it, but the opposite is also true: each time you miss, it becomes easier to miss again.

HABITS

At the 2007 National Speakers Bureau Convention in Orlando, Florida, the topic being talked about most frequently was author Jeffrey Gitomer.

Gitomer had done a seminar for Microsoft, and the company had ordered 6,000 autographed books for the event—5,000 copies of *Little Green Book of Getting Your Way* and 1,000 of *Little Black Book of Connections.* Gitomer's office in Charlotte had rented a truck and delivered the books so that those attending the seminar did not have to wait for them.

His habit of going the extra mile was well rewarded by seminar offers and orders for books from large corporations worldwide.

Study the habits of great men and women and you will discover that developing the right habits has played an incalculable part in their success.

Whether the habits you develop are good or bad, they define who you are and what you are capable of.

Remember that habits are formed by mental suggestions and persistence.

During my many years of studying success principles, I have found that good habits are easier to form and keep once you have a purpose for which you have a deep passion. I think you will discover the same in your life.

We can discover that what we desire in life is obtainable if we are willing to pay the price. This is true whatever the goal may be, whether it is financial security or some other milepost we wish to reach. We will reach our goal only if we are willing to pay the price. Discipline in our lives is a necessity if we are to reach goals that are worthy of our time and efforts. Do not expect to get what you want without paying the price. This is a very simple but important lesson.

Someone who makes a commitment to a worthy cause and persists will discover that her accomplishment will exceed the results of hundreds of less fortunate souls who lack persistence and quit when they face the least resistance. You need to practice persistence until persistence becomes a habit of yours.

You have the choice of making a habit of persistence or making a habit of quitting.

It was Vince Lombardi, coach of the Green Bay Packers, who said, "Winning is not a sometime thing; it's an all time thing. You don't win once in a while; you don't do things right once in a while; you do them right all the time. Winning is a habit. Unfortunately, so is losing."

Giving better service than others will put you ahead in your field. The results may not show up after one day, one week, or one month, but giving better service over a period of time will provide dividends. The job you are doing does not matter—whether you are a waiter or a banker, your efforts will not go unrewarded for long. The law of compensation is as natural and works as dependably as the law of gravity.

In the mid–1970s, I was employed as vice president of a new community bank that was very profitable. A local coal boom had helped the new bank to grow very fast. The bank had been founded by local men, most of whom were in the coal business, and they decided to sell the bank to one of the state's largest banks, receiving a very profitable return on their investment.

When a bank is sold to another bank, the deal must receive regulatory approval and then be reviewed by the U.S. Justice Department for possible violation of antitrust statutes. The decision is purely speculation as to whether or not competition will be affected by the merger.

Our bank was only a $40 million institution with two locations, yet the Justice Department challenged the merger, notifying us by phone the Friday before the Monday when the merger was to take place. The bank hired a local attorney, Don Pippin, and at the initial hearing in federal court, the Justice Department had about 20 people representing it, including attorneys, assistants, stenographers, and others. The banks that were seeking to merge hired a very large, prestigious law firm located in the nation's capital.

The lawsuit required thousands of hours of labor by bank employees to satisfy the government's request for information. I personally made trips to the Washington, DC, law firm to work on the case.

In the end, the federal court ruled in favor of the banks that wanted to merge and against the Justice Department. That was not the end of our problems because after the Justice Department lost the case, it had months to appeal, and rather than letting us know whether or not it intended to appeal the ruling, it left us in limbo until the period in which it could appeal had expired. The Justice Department could have notified the banks that it had no intention of appealing the case, but it did not.

The merger took place, and I retained my title as vice president and was offered a position as a commercial loan officer with the large bank. It was a very important position dealing with large commercial customers.

While I was employed as a commercial loan officer, I was approached and offered a job as chief executive officer of a federal savings and loan that was in severe financial trouble. The results were fantastic, but when I had been on the job for less than a year, I was indicted by the Justice Department and charged with having insider information and soliciting stockholders to purchase the stock of the bank that had previously employed me.

Normally, the court system tells us that we are innocent until proven guilty, but I was working in a bank whose deposits were federally insured, and I was not able to work once I had been indicted. Making headlines in this manner was not a lot of fun. My daughter was attending college, and a professor asked her about the indictment.

However, the indictment made me a much stronger person and helped me realize that anything less than death can be dealt with if you maintain your composure and do not bury your head in the sand.

A friend and local lawyer, Don Earles, gave me valuable advice and connected me to Don Huffman, a lawyer and former federal prosecutor in a city three hours away.

The antitrust case had identified the time of the first discussion of a possible bank merger, and I had purchased stock after that discussion. However, I had not known of the possible merger when I bought the stock, and I had not solicited to purchase it. A friend who was the founder and chairman of a bank in a nearby town had purchased stock in our bank. Before recording the stock in his name, he came into our bank and offered it to me. I simply withdrew money from my savings and bought the stock from him.

After the federal indictment, I obtained a letter from the gentleman affirming that I had not solicited to purchase the stock, and my lawyer met with federal prosecutors, who offered to reduce the charge from a felony with a possible long prison term and large fine to a misdemeanor with a small fine. I politely refused.

A few days later, the Justice Department realized its error and dropped all charges, and I returned to work after only a few days' absence.

The final result was that I was out $3,000 in attorney's fees, which I claimed as a deduction on my federal income tax. I wrote a note and quoted the tax code, and the expense was not questioned on my tax return.

There is a tremendous lesson in this: that those in positions of power can be proved wrong, and you should not panic if you are wrongly accused. If you are in the right, confront the problem, use the resources available to you, hold up your head, and persist until you succeed.

In the recent case at Duke University in which some members of the lacrosse team had felony charges brought against them by a very dishonest prosecutor who was seeking publicity to aid him in his election to public office, the prosecutor knew that the changes were false. The results were that the team, which was a contender for a national championship, was suspended for the season. A large number of professors from Duke signed a letter condemning the boys. When the truth came out, the fact that the rogue prosecutor had withheld information that proved their innocence caused the prosecutor to lose his job and his law license and to face charges himself. A settlement was reached with the students that reportedly cost Duke several million dollars. The news of the Duke case reminded me of my own legal bout, which happened about 25 years ago.

I am reminded of the words of the German philosopher Nietzsche, "that which does not kill you makes you stronger."

> *You gain strength, courage and confidence by*
> *every experience in which you really stop to look*
> *fear in the face. You are able to say to yourself,*
> *"I have lived through this horror. I can take the*
> *next thing that comes along." You must do the*
> *thing you think you cannot do.*
> —ELEANOR ROOSEVELT

Perseverance demonstrates that success may not come easily. Here is where you have a chance to belong to the 5 percent who are truly successful rather than the 95 percent who only dream of true success. The word *perseverance* tells you that hard work is required along with discipline and overcoming adversity, all of which will require you to never, never give up on your goals.

You will find that perseverance is much easier when you have selected your purpose in life. Here is where it is essential that you love what you are doing, have a passion for it, and have a belief that you will reach your goal. You will be less likely to give up when you are going after something you care about and doing what you love to do.

9

FRUGALITY AND
SELF-RELIANCE

*If you do not conquer self, you will be conquered
by others.*

—NAPOLEON HILL

**When your income from investments exceeds
your income from your job, you can
consider yourself wealthy.**

E VEN IF YOU use your skills and hard work to make a good income,
the seed of success will not be in you unless you learn to save
part of your earnings.

If you cannot save a portion of your income when you are not making a lot of money, you are likely to find that it is no easier to save when your income increases. It is easy to tell yourself, "Someday, when I make more money, I will have money to save." The problem with that thinking is that "someday" is not a part of the calendar. It is a polite way of lying to yourself to get yourself off the hook.

Saving money is a habit, and the statement that good habits are formed by repeating an act over and over until it becomes a part of each of us is true. The opposite side is that bad habits are acquired in the same manner.

FRUGALITY

When R.J., a young finance major at a large university, was asked by his mother, "R.J., you have a good job at the golf course for the summer. Why don't you just eat at the clubhouse?," R.J. replied, "Two reasons, Mom: first, the food is expensive, and second, if I stop to go into the clubhouse to eat, I have to clock out, and I won't get as many hours or tips." Now that's being frugal.

Say what you are going to do, then just do what you said.

I have found that many people say they will attend meetings or make a list of promises, yet fail to keep them. These failures to keep promises may seem unimportant, but when they accumulate over a period of time, they will help define you. It is like attending a meeting where someone you know says, "Everybody is here but Bill, and I talked to him and he said he would try to make the meeting." Don't fall into the habit of telling someone you will try to do something—either you will or you will not.

One day I got a call from Shane Morand regarding a potential book deal that would prove to be very beneficial to the Napoleon Hill Foundation. Let me share with you a little background on the origination of the foundation's business relationship with Morand's company, Organo Gold.

About two years ago, a young man named Scott VanGemert attended an open house at the Napoleon Hill World Learning Center, located at Purdue University-Calumet in Hammond, Indiana. Scott is a marketing guru, and he was doing work for the founder of a new sales organization, Bernie Chua. Scottie had become friends with Judith Williamson, the director of the World Learning Center, and Uriel "Chino" Martinez. Scott was a follower of the philosophy of success as taught by the Napoleon Hill Foundation.

It was only natural that a business relationship developed between Organo Gold and the Napoleon Hill Foundation because Organo Gold's salespeople had heard the sales trainers espouse the principles Napoleon Hill had studied and written about more than 100 years ago.

Shane told me that he had discussed having a business organization with a system that could not fail. I said, "Shane, the foundation has a book with the title of *The Success System That Never Fails* by

W. Clement Stone, who was chairman of the board of the Napoleon Hill Foundation and was responsible for getting the foundation into good financial condition." Shane remarked that he had not read the book, and I told him that I would send him a copy. Not only did I tell him that I would send him a copy of the book, but I told him that I would also send him a copy of *Napoleon Hill's Golden Rules*, published just last year. *Golden Rules* is a book composed of articles that Hill wrote between 1919 and 1923 for magazines that he owned. The books were sent by FedEx overnight.

What made the idea of a huge business contract with the Organo Gold organization possible was that it wanted to have a collectors' edition of *Think and Grow Rich!*, both in book and in audio, done in time to present it to the company's sales associates at an upcoming conference at the Ritz-Carlton in Jamaica. Not only were the officers of Organo Gold followers of Napoleon Hill's success philosophy, but they wanted to share it with other members of their organization. Not only were they willing to invest a considerable amount of money, but they did not seek a profit—only to expose their people to Hill and to raise money for the Napoleon Hill World Learning Center.

When I made the expense-paid trip to Jamaica with Judy, Uriel, and Scott, we attended a wonderful event. When Shane introduced me to the 800 attendees, he told them that I had told him that I would send the books and I had, and that even though he lived in Canada, he got them the next day. Shane explained to the crowd that not only had I done what I said, but I had also written him a card telling him that I liked his enthusiasm and included the Ralph Waldo Emerson quote that "nothing great was ever achieved without enthusiasm."

Remember that not only is intention worthless, but each time you disclose your intentions and fail to act, you are creating a pattern that will become a habit if you repeat it. You know that first we make the habits, and then the habits make us.

Intentions apply not only to business but, even more important, to one's personal life. Intending to make your child's Little League game, school function, or other event, then failing to attend, creates disappointment that can damage the parent-child relationship. The same can be said of intentions with a spouse, friend, or any other person in one's life.

Webster's *New World Dictionary* gives the definition of self-reliance as reliance on one's own judgment or abilities.

One of the best habits that a person can learn is being self-reliant. I don't mean that there is anything wrong with getting others to help you accomplish what you are trying to get done. I mean learning to do more based on your own judgment or abilities, as the dictionary describes.

Over and over, I have seen people who have a good job and a good income get into financial trouble for several reasons, including the inability to avoid delaying purchases. They accumulate debt for services that they could have performed themselves or could have delayed until they had saved enough cash and therefore avoided debt.

My parents were married in the middle of the Great Depression and, like many others at the time, were self-reliant out of necessity.

The lesson on self-reliance served them well throughout their lives. My father, who had only a seventh-grade education and was an underground coal miner, was one of the smartest people I was ever around. Survival was a lesson that had been well learned.

When World War II broke out, my parents moved to Norfolk, Virginia, where Dad worked in the shipyards and Dad and Mom kept boarders. In 1945, when the war ended, they moved back to southwest Virginia, and he returned to the coal mines, where he knew he could make a living. By this time, there were four boys in the family, Bob, Jerry, Danny, and me. A sister, Bernetta, came later, after four tough boys, and was the apple of my dad's eye.

Dad was self-reliant, no doubt from the lessons he learned from being raised during the Depression. While making about $14.00 per day, he was able to purchase one-half interest in 160 acres with Lee, his oldest brother.

While working the evening shift in the coal mines, 3 p.m. to 11 p.m., Dad got up in the morning and worked on the farm until it was time to go back to the mines. He continued this pattern for years, and he never once asked for government assistance, such as farm subsidies. When a coal mine was worked out and he faced the loss of his job, Dad simply looked until he found a job; he never once asked for public assistance, such as unemployment benefits or the government surplus food that was readily available. Once Dad was seriously injured by a rock fall in the mines and, while he was on crutches, could not pass the company doctor's physical. As a solution, he took a job driving a truck at much lower wages until his health improved and he was no longer on crutches.

Being self-reliant means being in control, and that means being financially responsible. Being in control is a behavioral trait and has very little to do with education.

Dad never owed more than $4,000, and that was to build a three-bedroom brick house; he paid off the loan over a two-year period.

When the house was built, a problem arose: good water could not be obtained. The solution was an excellent example of personal initiative, which is simply doing what needs to be done.

About a mile below the new house was a "freshwater" spring, where, as in the Bible, cool water came forth from the rocks. Again without the aid of the government, water departments, public authority, or any other organization whatsoever, Dad devised a plan to get water to the new house. First he built a springhouse with blocks that contained the water rather than letting it run off. He ordered an electric pump from a mail-order company, then he asked Bob, Jerry, Danny, and me to dig a ditch from the spring to the new house.

The ditch had to be dug about two feet deep to prevent the water in the water lines from freezing, and we had only hand tools. Once we got the ditch dug as far as the highway, we were presented with what looked like a big problem for four young boys: we had to dig through U.S. 23. Before the interstates were developed, this was the major highway going from Michigan all the way to Florida, passing through Virginia, where we lived, along the way.

The highway that we needed to dig a three-foot ditch through had thousands of cars passing over it 24 hours a day, and the only tools we had were hand tools: picks and shovels. We made a homemade barrier on one lane, forcing the traffic on that lane to drive off the asphalt road while we dug. At nightfall, we would fill the ditch back up so that both lanes could travel in order to prevent accidents. Early in the morning we would rake the dirt out and dig until the ditch was deep enough, then we repeated the process on the other side until we had dug a ditch and installed a water line and an electric cord.

Later, the Virginia Transportation Department came by and complained because the dirt would settle, leaving a rough spot in the road. Nevertheless, the transportation department sent men to fix the break in the pavement that we had created.

More than 50 years have passed, and the water is still flowing to the house my parents built.

You might ask, "Why tell this story?" To me, the answer is very simple: because it helps teach the habit of becoming self-reliant. Becoming self-reliant gives you confidence in yourself. Whether the obstacle you are facing is small or is larger than digging a one-mile ditch with hand tools and crossing a major U.S. highway, you will learn that a chore once begun is one-half done.

Most avid readers of self-help books are familiar with Ralph Waldo Emerson's "Essay on Compensation." Emerson also wrote an essay on self-reliance. At the end of that essay, he wrote that external events can raise your spirits, but "Nothing can bring you peace but yourself. Nothing can bring you peace but the triumph of principles."

Self-reliance will help you, as it has helped me, to learn that challenges don't seem like challenges if you know where you are going and are determined to get there.

The importance of becoming self-reliant and what the positive results of this habit teach cannot be overemphasized. Learn this lesson and turn challenges into opportunities.

10

LEARNING FROM OTHERS

Keep your face to the sunshine and you cannot see the shadow.

— HELEN KELLER

WHEN I THINK of my childhood days, I think mostly of the happy events that have taken place in my life. Sometimes thoughts of my childhood seem like something that I read about in a book in my first year of elementary school, which had six grades in a two-room school.

The school had two teachers, Patton Edwards and Goldie Ball. My first memory of school was lunch. My mother filled a metal pail (which syrup had come in) with milk and cornbread and dropped spoons into the milk and bread. One of my older brothers—either Bobby or Jerry—would place the container in a small creek in front of the school. The water helped keep the milk cold. At lunchtime, we removed the pail from the small creek. The milk and bread made a good lunch. Often we would have biscuits with ham or jelly prepared by our mother. The school had outdoor restrooms with no running water.

Some of the things that seemed so difficult back then are funny today when I reflect back on them. For example, when I was in the first grade at Dog Branch Elementary, one of the problems was getting water from the school's well.

The school had only a well for drinking water, and the bigger boys would draw water from the well using a rope and pulley attached to a well bucket. I realized very quickly that I had a problem, as the school did not furnish paper cups to drink from. I noticed that the other students were taking a sheet of paper and folding it to form a cup. The only thing I needed was someone to show me how to fold the paper to form the cup so that it would hold the water. I persuaded an older boy to demonstrate the cup process, and this became an early lesson in learning from others.

A good friend of mine, the late Charlie "Tremendous" Jones, frequently said we are who we are because of the people we associate with and the books we read.

You will find that people who are successful are usually very eager to help you as you search for plans to reach your goals.

We should use the lives of other people as examples so that we may be inspired by their accomplishments and model our lives on theirs.

Not only can we learn from others, but successful people get pleasure from helping others, and you will discover that they do just that.

Our lives go through three stages: the first is learning, the second is earning, and the third is sharing. This third stage should be the best stage of one's life. This is the stage in which you create your legacy.

In 1999, I was working as a banker and teaching a class called Keys to Success. I had been instrumental in getting this class started at a local college that had been organized in 1955 with a $10,000 grant from the Virginia State Legislature. As a member of the college's board, I attended the 2005 graduation. I heard a speaker remark that this $10,000 was probably the best money the legislature had ever spent. The college was the only branch of the University of Virginia and was then known at Clinch Valley College.

In 1999, a small group of local citizens, all alumni of the college, went to the state capitol in Richmond to urge the legislature to change the name from Clinch Valley College to something that would show the college's connection to the University of Virginia. I was among this group.

To most of those involved, the task seemed to be insurmountable for several reasons. First, the University of Virginia was founded by our third president, Thomas Jefferson, and is one of the top-ranked colleges in the United States. Many of the people at the university did not want a small college in the mountains of southwestern Virginia to be confused with the university. Even the board of the University of Virginia was very much opposed to the idea, as were many of the personnel connected to Clinch Valley College.

Those of us who were pressing for it considered a name change to be a marketing masterpiece. A University of Virginia diploma would make it much easier for students to market themselves upon graduation. Would-be employers outside the area probably would not recognize the name of Clinch Valley College, but even an employer in Brazil would be likely to recognize University of Virginia. In recruiting students for the college, the name change would be heaven-sent.

The name change required legislative approval from the Commonwealth of Virginia. Don Pippin, William Sturgill, J. Jack Kennedy, and I made a visit to Richmond to try to convince the members of the legislature of the importance of the name change. Without exception, it seemed that the elected officials had already been pressured by different people on behalf of the University of Virginia to resist any change. Here was all the political might of the prestigious folks associated with the University of Virginia against a little-known college in the mountains. Talk about David against Goliath.

The Board of Regents of the University of Virginia, headed by a prestigious lawyer from one of Virginia's largest law firms, was strongly opposed (and I use the word *strongly* in a mild sense), as were the overwhelming majority of the University of Virginia alumni. Even many of the students and professors at Clinch Valley College did not want a name change. What they failed to see was the tremendous benefit of changing from an unknown name to one that showed an association with the University of Virginia.

BELIEF

J. Jack Kennedy was a young lawyer serving a term in the Virginia legislature in 1991 when he developed a strong belief that he could get the name of Clinch Valley College (the only branch of the University of Virginia) changed to recognize its relationship with the University of Virginia, which was founded by Thomas Jefferson, our third president.

Jack had the belief that changing the school's name would be a monumental accomplishment in terms of marketing prestige and the ability to attract students.

While Jack did not succeed at this during his term in the legislature, he never gave up on his belief. He worked with others, including William Wampler, who defeated him in his bid for reelection. The legislature changed the school's name to the University of Virginia's College at Wise in 1999, and the change has been of tremendous value in terms of attracting students and fund-raising.

We are reminded of Frank Lloyd Wright's statement: "The thing always happens that you really believe in; and the belief in a thing makes it happen."

J. Jack Kennedy, an attorney and a former member of the Virginia House of Delegates and the Virginia State Senate, knew most of the members of the legislature, which helped our cause. Kennedy first proposed a name change in 1991 while he was serving in the Virginia legislature. State Senator William Wampler, who oddly enough defeated Kennedy for the senate seat after a redistricting pitted them against each other, led the fight by his sponsorship of the bill. The defeat in 1991 was a lesson in politics.

Once we had presented our case, I was amazed at the help we received from others. One of my pleasanter experiences was meeting Emily Couric, the sister of Katie Couric of ABC News. She was extra caring. It was easy to be impressed by Ms. Couric. In addition to her striking good looks, she had compassion for our cause, even though she was pressured by the University of Virginia alumni and the university's board. Ms. Couric, as state senator, represented the area where the University of Virginia was located. I thought that she would one day become attorney general of Virginia and be a serious challenger for the governor's office. Unfortunately, her untimely death cut short her glittering political career.

Don Pippin, a good old country lawyer, made a speech to the senate committee, and the members were astounded by the energy that they had been confronted with. The name change passed the legislative committee—surprising a lot of people. The next move was approval by the legislature itself.

Of course, a great deal of work was done through individual meetings with the members of the Virginia Senate, such as Yvonne Miller from Norfolk. Being a member of a minority group, she sided with the "little people" in the cause, and her help was just outstanding. The final vote to approve the name change was 35 yeas and 5 nays. The college's name became the University of Virginia's College at Wise. The name generally used today is UVA-Wise.

This process of changing the name of the college made use of many of the principles of success. First, those who wanted a name change had a burning desire to achieve this goal. They believed that their trip to the Virginia State Capitol would not be in vain. Teamwork was demonstrated from the first. On the automobile trip, my hands-free cell phone was in constant use, running up a bill of several hundred dollars, because the group knew what needed to be done and had a vision.

In a recent meeting, former chancellor Ernie Ern stated that he could not believe the positive impact the name change had had on the university. Enrollment, fund-raising, ranking, and other ways of measuring the college's success have all improved dramatically. The whole event shows how people who are successful are often willing to help others for just causes.

We must enlist the help of others and remember John Donne's words: "No man is an island." It is essential that you get help from others and likewise extend help when you are in a position to do so.

Successful people are often in a position to give tremendous help to others, and many are willing to do so. Successful individuals have made their own accomplishments possible by getting others to help them, so when they, in turn, are in a position to assist others, they will usually be glad to do so.

During my high school days, I used to cut mining timber, and I still remember the numbers. The selling price of timber was 8¢ per foot, and the timbers were 7 feet in length (the height of underground coal mines), which equaled 56¢ per piece of timber. Every time my two older brothers, Bobby and Jerry, and I cut a hundred timbers (with a handsaw), we had $56 to divide among us. Our younger brother, Danny, brought water to us and was paid. Talk about self-employed entrepreneurs! We were that, although we did not know what the word meant.

Thanks to my various enterprises while I was still in high school, after my older brother finished high school, took a job, and got married, I was able to loan him the money for the down payment on his first house.

While I was in junior college, I worked several jobs. I drove a school bus, getting $76 per month, and I worked at a service station on the weekends, pumping gas, changing oil, washing vehicles, and doing whatever else was needed. The service station job paid 75¢ per hour, and I was very thankful for that. I worked for Bob Adkins at the local Phillips 66 station, and Bob is a good friend today. I learned a lot about people on the job.

What I learned was that each job was truly a blessing and paid dividends quickly, but also the invaluable lesson that one should be committed to the job that one was engaged in at the moment and always be proud of what one accomplished through hard work. Each of my brothers and I learned the lesson of persistence, which has remained with us through our adult years.

No job should be considered beneath you; each should be seen as a starting point. Menial jobs seem unimportant only when you accept them as dead-end jobs and have no hope for a better future.

A desire that is a passion will allow you to accomplish more than you would if you had a so-what attitude toward opportunities that present themselves. Also, you can create better opportunities by being alert to the possibilities that exist. Allow me to give you an example.

One summer, I overheard the owner of a small pony coal mine talk about buying mining steel from a coal mine near the West Virginia line. A pony mine is an underground coal mine that used ponies to pull coal cars (small wagonlike carts) from the location where the coal was being dug. The coal was loaded onto the coal cars (usually by hand labor using a large shovel). The work was dirty, very hard, and dangerous, and it offered only a poor chance of getting ahead. The cars rode on steel rails that were like railroad tracks, except much smaller; the tracks made the cars much easier to pull than trying to get them to move through dirt, mud, and water.

On weekends, my brother and I would go to the mine, feed the ponies hay and grain, and see that they had fresh water. R. O. Goad, the owner of the mine, often bought steel tracks from other mines that were going out of business. He either used the steel in his coal mine or sold it for a profit. In this case, my brothers and I volunteered to go to the West Virginia mine and "pull the steel" that Mr. Goad had purchased. My brother Bobby was 18, Jerry was 16, and I was 14.

We went to the mine in a large truck. Once we reached the mine, the task was simple, yet very difficult. There was no electricity underground, so we had to use lamps to see. The job was to pull out the rails, which were 15 to 24 feet in length.

The first problem was that the rails were bolted together, and, since they were underground and there was water and mud, the bolts that held them together had rusted. Using hand tools, we were able to loosen some of the bolts; others had to be sawed off with a hand file.

The next problem was dragging the rails outside in order to load them on the truck. Dragging steel rails for some distance was very hard. The coal mine was about 40 inches high, which meant that we could not stand up, and this made the job more difficult.

An old, bald-headed man (as nearly as I can remember, his last name was Miller) saw the struggle my brothers and I were having, and though he did not physically help, he offered a solution. Each rail had holes in the ends so that the rails could be bolted together. Mr. Miller said that in his younger days, he had done what we were attempting to do. He suggested that we get small ropes, put one end through the holes, tie a knot, and then use the rope to pull the rail out.

I can still recall how much easier the job of pulling the rails to the outside of the underground mine and to where the rails were loaded onto the truck became.

Throughout life, each of us will encounter hundreds of instances in which we can use others' experiences to our advantage.

Most young people have received some of their best lessons from their parents. Often these lessons are things their parents did that helped them create their own legacy. These were tremendous lessons, even though we may realize this only when we reflect upon our childhood days.

First, let me tell you about my father. He was a remarkable person, although he had only a seventh-grade education. I can remember so many acts of kindness that he did for others without expecting anything in return. For example, when cold weather came in the late fall, there would be a "hog killing." This event began by lighting fires and heating water to pour on the carcasses in order to soften the hair, and younger family members would help to remove the hair by scraping it off with a big butcher knife.

Once the hogs had been slaughtered and the intestines had been removed, the head and feet were cut off. Next, the body was cut into various pieces. Some of the meat was cooked, some was made into sausages, and some was used for pork chops and other cuts. Finally, the only body parts left were the head and feet. Our family did not use the head or the feet, so Dad would take them to one of the nearby coal camps. In the camps were members of several minority groups who had moved there seeking employment.

One hog-killing day, I went with my dad, and he explained what he was doing. He drove to a coal camp in Clinchco and stopped when he saw a woman out in front of a company house. Dad asked her if she would like some hog head and feet, and her reply was, "Mister, I'd love to have 'em, but work is slow in the coal camps and we don't have any money." Dad told her that she didn't need any money. He gave her and her neighbors all the pig heads and feet that were left from the hog killing earlier in the day.

My dad would not go past a person who was hitchhiking when he was traveling near home or pass by a vehicle that had broken down.

I remember one winter Dad was working in a deep mine in Carbo, Virginia, and was on the evening shift, which was from 3 p.m. to 11 p.m. It was about midnight, and when he was driving home, he came through the town of Wise and picked up a young man who was hitchhiking. It was deathly cold, and the young man had been on the street for a long time. Dad not only picked him up but brought him home.

Our family at the time was made up of my parents, three brothers, a sister, and me, all living in a four-room house. The house had two bedrooms, a kitchen, and a living room, with no bathroom.

I awoke the next morning with one of my brothers and a grown-up stranger. He must have been deathly tired, as Dad and Mom let him sleep late. When the young man awoke, Mom served him gravy, biscuits, and bacon. Dad then insisted on driving him to the next town and told him that if he had trouble getting a ride, he could go into a business in the town of Pound, Virginia, and get warm. This is the kind of deed that leaves a legacy through acts of kindness bestowed on others.

My mother, who is past 89 years old, may have had only a seventh-grade education, but, like my dad, she often sees things she can do for those around her on a daily basis. Mom uses the phone to check on elderly friends and neighbors to see if they are OK and to see if they have taken their medicine or if they need any help. She still visits nursing homes on a daily basis and never misses a chance to deliver food when neighbors or friends have a sickness or death in the family. You don't need to have money to leave a legacy; you can do acts of kindness instead.

Hopefully each of us can make a difference by learning from others concerning ways in which we can help those who are in need. I have learned that one does not have to look very far to see someone on whom he can make a positive impact.

11

MENTORS

*Seek you counsel of the aged for their eyes have
looked on the faces of the years and their ears have
hardened to the voices of Life. Even if their counsel
is displeasing to you, pay heed to them.*

— KAHLIL GIBRAN 1883–1931

Mentors are priceless.

I N 1975, I was branch manager for a consumer finance company
in eastern Tennessee. It was a pleasant town to live in, with major
employers like Eastman Chemicals, defense contractors, glass manu-
facturers, and a publishing firm, which meant that there were a lot of

good-paying jobs. This is important if you are lending money because when there are good jobs, the borrowers are easier to qualify and to collect from.

Being a branch manager had been good to me. While I had managed four different offices, I had had to move only twice, and I had been able to get a bachelor of science degree with a major in accounting and a minor in business by attending East Tennessee State University at night.

One day I received a call from a banker in my hometown, who suggested that I should apply for a job in a new bank that had been open for about one year. The bank had been organized by a group of local men, most of them connected to the coal-mining industry in the Appalachian Mountains. I told the banker that I would be glad to come for an interview on a Saturday, but it would not be right for me to seek other employment on a day when I was being paid by another financial institution.

I was interviewed by James A. Brown, who before the age of 30 had helped to organize a local community bank. Jim, as he was known, had a college degree in engineering and was employed in the coal business when he decided to go into business for himself. There was a coal boom during the seventies, and many of the miners had become very wealthy in a short period of time.

During the interview, which took place in Jim's office and not at the bank, Jim said, "You know, if you work a few minutes more one day by coming in early and staying a little later than everybody else, it probably won't make much difference. If you do this every day for a month, it might make a little difference, but if you do it every day for several years, you will no doubt be in a class by yourself." I was already doing this in my career, but after all these years, I still remember the advice that Jim gave me. We have remained friends, and we stay in touch. Jim is one of the most intelligent people I have been fortunate enough to be around.

Advice from people like Jim is priceless.

Another person I look to for advice is Dr. Joseph C. Smiddy, known by his friends as "Papa Joe." You don't have to be around Papa Joe for more than a moment to be attracted by his warm, gentle smile and his sense of humor.

More than any other person, Dr. Smiddy is responsible for the tremendous success of the University of Virginia-Wise. The college was organized in 1954 as Clinch Valley College, a two-year institution. The property had been used for indigent people during the Great Depression; it was referred to as a "poor farm," because the people living there helped raise crops for food. So when the college was opened, many people called it Poor Farm University, or PFU.

Dr. Smiddy served on the board of the bank where I was president and chief executive officer. He had the necessary traits to be an excellent mentor. Doc was well educated, and his public relations skills were the absolute best. In action, he was kind and friendly to everyone he met, no matter what their social or financial position. Above all, Doc had the one quality that ranks above all other traits, and that was his integrity.

I remember one time a potential problem developed at the bank. At a board meeting where the problem was being discussed, Doc said to me, "I will stand by you if you are right, but if you are wrong, you will stand alone." When you know you are right, what more could you ask for than to be told that?

You do not have to agree with your mentors on subjects such as politics and religion, but their honesty must be above reproach.

The interesting thing about mentors is that you will find them approachable and willing to share their advice with you. Most successful people have an overwhelming desire to give back to help others. Don't be afraid to seek help from others, especially in areas where you lack expertise and you know others who have the particular knowledge that you lack.

If you are in business for yourself or you have another business outside of your present employer, it would be wise for you to seek out an attorney for advice. If you can develop a mentor relationship with him, it would be excellent.

When I took the job as president of that local bank nearly 30 years ago, I was fortunate enough to meet such a person.

William J. Sturgill was a very successful lawyer with various real estate and coal-mining investments. He was the son of a coal miner and had been raised in circumstances very much like mine. After his discharge from the army, he was in the first class (1954) at Clinch Valley College. Later on, he taught school, operated an insurance office, and finished law school.

Bill did the legal work for the creation of the bank, arranging for its organization, selling bank stock, and obtaining a charter from the state of Virginia. He served as chairman of the board until the bank was sold to a group of investors.

Bill and I would usually have lunch together one day a week, discussing banking and other items of mutual interest. One day Bill mentioned that a friend of ours, Darrell Freddie Dean, a local CPA, wanted to start a cable TV company. I was invited to invest, and we agreed not to borrow money, but to put in our own money instead. The cable company operated for eight years and was sold to one of the largest cable companies in the United States. The investment paid a tremendous return, which was made possible by the relationships that we had developed over the years.

Choose a mentor or mentors, try never to disappoint her, and exhibit the highest degree of integrity, and you will be surprised by how many extremely successful people are willing to share their knowledge.

MENTORS

We can learn from others—even monkeys can do that. A mentor is an advisor who can be trusted to help one with one's individual development.

Jim Stovall is an excellent example of mentoring. First, Jim had his own mentors when he was growing up in Tulsa, Oklahoma. While attending Oral Roberts University, Jim discovered that he was losing his eyesight as a result of macular degeneration, which has no cure.

Instead of becoming a burden on society, Jim was mentored and became very successful selling stock by phone. He received many requests to speak and explain his success and became a highly sought-after speaker. As he developed his talents, he turned to writing; he has written 16 books and has become a bestselling author with millions of copies sold. Today Jim is a mentor to many people, and his desire to give back is amazing.

The reason you will be attracted to successful people is because of Ralph Waldo Emerson's law of compensation. Authors more than 100 years ago wrote about the law of compensation, which simply states that if you do excellent work, either you will be recognized by your employer and given salary increases and promotions, or another employer will discover your talents and hire you away from your present employer. This was what happened to me when I got into the banking business. I had worked in the consumer finance industry for about 13 years, and I had earned an excellent reputation for my work. The new bank was only a year old and was terribly deficient in qualified personnel, especially in the area of lending and collections, which was my area of expertise.

I have never had to seek full-time employment since I first became employed. Employers will seek you out if you make your skills the best in your particular line of work.

You will be able to market yourself with very little effort if you choose to associate with other successful people. Success attracts success, and failure attracts failure. Like attracts like, and that is not a new principle, in spite of recent books written on the subject.

My dear mother used to tell my brothers and me, "Birds of a feather flock together." We probably pretended to not know what she meant, but her advice was as worthwhile then as it is today. We are all social creatures, and we easily take on the characteristics of those we spend our time with. Today, I recall the advice of the late Charlie "Tremendous" Jones, who said, "We will be the same in five years from now as we are today, except for two things, and those are the books we read and the people we meet."

While we can learn good traits from positive-minded
people, we need to remove ourselves from negative
people as much as possible. We become like those we
associate with most of the time.

The German poet Goethe wrote, "To know someone here or there
with whom you can feel there is understanding in spite of distances or
thoughts expressed—that can make life a garden."

In my circumstances, I have been blessed by being able to
get to know others, learn to understand them, and make lasting
friendships.

For example, the Napoleon Hill Foundation has done business
with SSI Corporation in Japan, founded and led by Tanaka Taka-aki.
Even though a great distance separates us, we are able to visit in person and by modern communication on a regular basis. To build and
maintain such a friendship is a priceless commodity.

Mr. Tanaka was born in Nakano, Tokyo, in 1945 and graduated
from the law department of Kokugakuin University. Later he held various important positions with the Japan Fair Trade Commission and
the Planning Department of Tokyo Land Corporation before found-
ing SSI Corporation as CEO and president in 1979.

From 1979 to 2007, Mr. Tanaka created a learning system that
he called the SSPS-V2 System and translated numerous works, including *The Napoleon Hill Program*. The development of the Hyper-
Listening machine was awarded a certificate of recognition by the
Guinness Book of World Records.

Mr. Tanaka is a noted author, and his works are centered on self-motivation, brainpower, and accelerated thinking. In another genre, he has written books on the Japanese and Tamil languages. His translated works cover a very wide range, from the inspirational writings of Napoleon Hill, including *Think and Grow Rich!*, to A *Dravidian Etymological Dictionary*. Mr. Tanaka was named an honorary trustee of the Napoleon Hill Foundation and in March 2003 became the first Japanese to receive a Napoleon Hill Gold Medal.

He is a true entrepreneur, and in 2004 he was among Japan's top 10 taxpayers for the fiscal year.

12

OPPORTUNITIES

To find out what one is fitted to do, and to secure
an opportunity to do it, is the key to happiness.

—JOHN DEWEY

I AM SURE you have heard that obstacles can be used as stepping-stones. I have been involved in real estate all of my adult life, and I have learned that the biggest opportunity that you can act on is a solution to someone else's problem.

About 15 years ago, two noted attorneys in my hometown had problems that led to the breakup of their law practice. The attorneys owned a tract of land located at a traffic light on a major four-lane highway, a highly visible location. It is said that there are three important things in real estate: "location, location, location." This property had it all.

Although the property had not been advertised, I knew of the attorneys' situation, and I thought that the timing was good and that I might be able to purchase the property. For any purchaser, the best opportunity occurs at a time when the seller wants or needs to sell. I made contact with one of the owners, who priced the property; I then made a counteroffer, and it was accepted. I purchased the land for about $150,000 and later sold it for $2 million, or a return of 1300 percent.

I relate this example not to show you what a fantastic deal my partners and I made when the property was purchased for a Walmart Supercenter, but to help you understand that something that is a problem for one person is an opportunity for others. Being alert for areas you are interested in that have problems will allow you to take the problem and create an opportunity.

While I was in banking, I once got word of 92 acres of land for sale in the Cumberland Gap area of Lee County, Virginia. This is an area known as the Wilderness Road, as Daniel Boone and his followers passed through it, helping to open up the new territory for settlers who were looking for adventure and a better future. The land is wooded and very rugged. This tract of land contained a mountain spring known to the locals as Blue Willow Spring.

Dr. Joseph Smiddy, known as Papa Joe, told me that people liked the water so well that those people who moved up north to seek employment would often come home to visit and fill up plastic jugs to take back up north.

I got interested in spring water several years ago, while I was in banking. I could see the public's increased need and desire for natural spring water to replace sugar-laden soft drinks. I began to read, study, and accumulate data on the spring water business, and I saw that Coca-Cola, Pepsi Cola, Nestlé, and other multibillion-dollar corporations were getting into the business. I won't go into detail about spring water, but a couple of facts I discovered were interesting. First, to be called spring water, the water needs to be bottled at the source (the spring where the water originates), and second, hauling water long distances is very expensive, so many different springs would be required to supply the United States with bottled water.

When my partners, Earl Wendell Barnette, Ben Sergent, and Milas Frank, and I found out that this 92-acre tract with a spring that was known to have supplied water to locals for more than a century could be purchased, the timing was excellent. An elderly couple with no children wanted to sell the property and give the proceeds to their nieces and nephews. This is just an example of being prepared and ready when one person's desire to sell becomes an opportunity for others. Of course, the transaction was a very good one for both parties.

The sellers got what they wanted, and we as purchasers got a good financial deal (otherwise I would not relate the story).

Studying changing trends and "getting in early" is a lesson that can pay off for you in both financial and personal satisfaction. Years ago, I was playing golf one day with Ben Sergent and Wendell Barnette, two of my longtime friends, partners, and golf buddies, and after we finished, we stopped at one of Wendell's convenience stores and bought some bottled water. One of Wendell's handymen saw us and said he could not believe that people would pay for water. This is just an example of the fact that some people can see opportunity and others cannot, or can see it only when it is too late to take advantage of it.

I could relate many more stories about opportunities, but I think you get the message: you need to be alert and prepared to act upon opportunities when they arise in your life.

Always keep paper and a pen close by. I often wake up with ideas on my mind. I at once take a legal pad and write down my thoughts while they are still new.

Once you have written down your thoughts, keep them on 3 × 5 cards where they are readily available. Only by keeping ideas nearby will you be likely to see opportunities that will help you to bring the ideas to completion.

Opportunities present themselves every day, and you can learn to be prepared to act. Remember, all the opportunities in the world are a blessing only to those who take action.

While I was in the banking business, I had plenty of people remind me of the time when they could have purchased the bank's stock for $3 a share; of course, they had not done so. Taking action would have given them about a 600 percent return on their investment. Of course, when you make any investment, you can lose part or all of your money, but calculating your risk and dividing it among different assets will help provide some protection.

This book is not a get-rich-quick manual, but it is intended to remind you that you should follow sound principles, educate yourself, and invest in what you understand; if you do not understand what you are investing in, leave the investment to others. If you are ever tempted to get rich quick, remember the verse from the Bible that says that if one is to get rich, get rich slowly. This is to help you not just get money but, much more important, obtain knowledge.

I have noticed that once you have a burning desire to accomplish something, you will start to see things coming to you that will greatly assist you in your pursuit of success.

Let me give you an example of what I mean when I say that you will start to notice things that you probably either did not notice or paid very little attention to previously.

Have you ever purchased a new car? Remember the time you purchased a new red Ford Mustang or a solid black BMW, and then all of a sudden you began to see cars just like the one you had recently purchased? It is not that they hadn't been there before, but that when you bought a car of a particular make and color, you started noticing other cars like yours. Most of them were probably already there.

You can relate this to opportunities. If your goal is to purchase and develop or sell real estate, you will notice possibilities to acquire real estate and make a good profit. Some of the potential deals that most people do not see can not only be profitable but make you a fortune.

When you have goals, you are likely to see many opportunities that you would not see otherwise.

When I was employed in the banking business as a CEO, I was already a devout reader of self-help books, biographies, autobiographies, and rags-to-riches stories like the Horatio Alger books for boys.

Because of my particular fondness for Napoleon Hill, I was invited to speak to the local historical society in Pound, Virginia. This location is near the place where Hill was born in 1883.

Speaking before a small group, I remarked that Napoleon Hill was born on the Pound River, near where Francis Gary Powers grew up. Powers became a world figure when his U-2 spy plane was shot down over the Soviet Union in 1960, and he parachuted out of the plane.

Powers was captured, put on public display, tried, and sentenced to a Soviet prison. This was during the Eisenhower administration and at the height of the Cold War. Powers had been recruited by the CIA (Central Intelligence Agency) to fly reconnaissance flights over the Soviet Union.

On May 1, 1960, Powers saw something that appeared to be a missile installation, and he flew below his normal altitude to take pictures of it. He was discovered by the Soviets, who fired a missile at him; it exploded, doing heavy damage to the lightweight spy plane. Powers, the only occupant, was forced to parachute.

The incident was of particular interest to me for several reasons. First, I knew Powers's father. He had often given me a ride in the morning when I hitchhiked to school. I grew up in the mountain area, and the school bus did not come by where I lived. Oliver Powers was very proud of his son, who after high school attended a college in eastern Tennessee and upon graduation joined the U.S. Air Force. From the air force, Powers was recruited by the CIA to conduct spy flights for the U.S. government.

On May 1, 1960, Powers left the American base in Peshawar, Pakistan, on that fateful flight. Powers's father had told me that his son flew flights getting weather information. After Gary was sentenced to Soviet prison, Oliver Powers, who had been a coal miner but was then the owner of a shoe-repair shop, appealed to Nikita Khrushchev, the Soviet premier, asking him to be "fair to my boy."

He said he was sure that Khrushchev would listen to him, speaking as one former coal miner to another. A year and a half later, the United States managed to secure the younger Powers's release by exchanging him for a Soviet spy it had in prison whose cover name was Rudolf Abel.

After my talk, I was approached by Oliver Powers's daughter, who told me that she was a sister of Francis Gary Powers and gave me a picture of the former prisoner in his air force uniform.

Driving back home after the speech, I listened to a tape by W. Clement Stone. When I returned home, I picked up the legal pad that I keep on the nightstand next to my bed so that if I wake up with an idea, I can write it down. I wrote to the Napoleon Hill Foundation, which was located in Northbrook, Illinois, at the time and told of my interest in Napoleon Hill. Mr. Stone was chairman of the board at the time; Dr. Charlie Johnson was president, James Oleson was vice president, and Mike Ritt was executive director.

I received a letter from Mike Ritt inviting me to Chicago for a board of trustees meeting. I went to that meeting and waited until Mr. Stone was seated so that I could sit next to him. It was indeed a thrill to meet someone of Stone's stature. Here was a gentleman about 90 years old who was a living example of what was possible to accomplish in life. I had read Mr. Stone's story of being a six-year-old living on the rough side of Chicago.

Stone was often beaten up by the older boys over space on the streets to hawk newspapers. He finally went into a local restaurant while breakfast was being served; he was promptly escorted out of the eating establishment—but only after he had sold some of his newspapers, often getting tip money as well. Stone kept returning because being escorted from the restaurant was not as dangerous as being beaten up by the bigger boys on the street.

After he had been put out on the street several times, the customers took the young Stone's side and encouraged the owner to allow the budding entrepreneur and newspaper seller to remain inside to sell his papers.

Stone learned an important lesson in persistence and not giving up when faced with adversity. The lesson remained with Stone all his life, which was to the age of 100. When Stone died, he had planned a celebration of his life. I was fortunate enough to have been invited to attend this day of honor for a man who gave away up to $400 million to benefit humanity.

What started as a simple invitation to speak before a local historical group gave me a chance to create an opportunity that has helped the Napoleon Hill Foundation to generate millions of dollars, endow scholarships in honor of Napoleon Hill, and create a professorship at the University of Virginia-Wise in the name of Napoleon Hill.

Upon Mike Ritt's retirement, I was asked by the other trustees to become executive vice president (chief executive officer) of the Napoleon Hill Foundation. This is just an example of how you can create opportunity by taking steps to follow up on your imagination concerning what is possible.

Opportunities are often all around us, and sometimes the only decision to make is which one you want to pursue. Remember what Earl Nightingale once said, "We can do anything we want to do but we can't do everything." So study your opportunities and decide which ones you want to take after you have enough facts to go ahead.

Having been a banker for four decades, I still subscribe to the *Wall Street Journal*. Recently an article appeared on the front page of the *Journal* about a professor at the University of Tehran in Iran who had published Napoleon Hill's *Grow Rich with Peace of Mind*. The article went on to explain about the great interest the youth in Iran had in the self-help movement. I clipped and saved the article. To show how entrepreneurs think, Bob Johnson, our copyright attorney and a successful investor, also clipped the article and mailed it to me!

It could have been just an interesting article and ended there, but I saw an opportunity. I asked "Chino" Martinez, my administrative assistant, to go to Google and get me a contact for the Iranian professor, which he did. Next, Annedia Sturgill, my longtime executive assistant, sent an e-mail to the professor, which for some reason did not go through.

This could have been a place to stop, but it was just one step that did not work. The next step was to call the *Journal*'s news department to say that I was a subscriber, give them the name of the *Journal* correspondent, and ask how I could make contact. I was given the correspondent's e-mail address in Beirut, Lebanon. I promptly e-mailed her and advised her that I had read and enjoyed her published piece on the self-help movement in Iran, and that I wanted to contact the Tehran University professor. The next morning I had a response from her.

This follow-up to an opportunity will no doubt generate a large amount of money for the Napoleon Hill Foundation and make friends in another part of the world. Also, I remembered the motto of the Napoleon Hill Foundation: making the world a better place in which to live.

RESPONSIBILITY

Being responsible means completing a task in a satisfactory manner.

It is easy to find someone to blame when you are not successful. A young banker many years ago kept a sign on his desk with a simple message, "If it is to be, it is up to me." This means taking responsibility for yourself and looking into a mirror, knowing that you have done your best. Taking responsibility will allow you to live a life with few regrets.

As the chief executive of the foundation, I am invited to many functions and choose to attend some periodically. Several years ago I was invited to a meeting of the Guideposts organization in Cleveland, Ohio. Guideposts is a very prestigious group that is operated today by the successors of Rev. Dr. Norman Vincent Peale, the bestselling author of many books, but best known for *The Power of Positive Thinking*. This event was held in one of Cleveland's most famous hotels.

Each attendee was furnished with a name tag. For example, mine simply read, "Don Green, Wise, Virginia."

As we were seated at tables, we each introduced ourselves. The lady next to me said, "Where is Wise, Virginia?," and I replied that Wise was in the southwestern part of the state, in the Appalachian Mountains. The woman then asked, "Don't you have a lot of poverty where you live?" I replied, "Yes," trying to keep the conversation short, as people were being introduced and I felt it was rude to engage in conversation. The next comment was kind of like, "Can't somebody do something to help those poor people?"

Once we got a break, I turned toward the lady who kept talking about poverty in the Appalachian Mountains. I did not feel anger toward her, but only sympathy. No doubt this lady knew about poverty in the mountains where I live from old television programs like *The Beverly Hillbillies*, and *Green Acres* and documentaries such as the one by Rory Kennedy, daughter of Senator Robert Kennedy and niece of President John F. Kennedy. Most of the news has been exaggerated or focused on stories such as the Hatfield-McCoy feud.

I told the lady that when I arrived at the Cleveland airport, I had been picked up by a limousine that drove me downtown past the Cleveland Indians' baseball stadium to the hotel. I told her that on my trip into the city, I could see several people underneath one of the many bridges there, apparently *living* under the bridge. I further informed her that in our area, I had never seen a homeless person, and I believed that if such a person existed, neighbors would assist him. I ended my conversation, perhaps a little abruptly, by telling her that there were poor people and rich people living everywhere. My advice to her was, if she could just remember what I was telling her, that both poverty and riches were a product of the mind.

To the reader: please note that there is poverty in the Appalachian Mountains, as there is in every part of the world. The mountains have produced famous sports figures, such as All-American and former Green Bay Packers Super Bowl champion Carroll Dale, a personal friend of mine; Thomas Jones, another All-American and All-Pro football player; distinguished authors such as Adriana Trigiani; and superwealthy people whom, for personal reasons, I will not name for publication.

Both riches and poverty are truly products of the human mind. First we have a thought, then we have a plan for accomplishment, then we proceed to take action and persist until the desired results are obtained.

You probably have heard the saying, "The grass is greener on the other side—but you still have to mow it." No matter where you are, you will need to take the steps that every other successful person has taken. You may do it faster, or you may be slower in realizing your dream. The main points are that the dreams are yours and that, if you need help, you should seek out wise mentors and follow your dreams on the road to success.

You are the only person who can make you a success or a failure; the decision is yours and yours alone.

If you are successful, remember that somewhere, sometime, someone gave you a lift or an idea that started you in the right direction. Remember, also, that you are indebted to life until you help some less fortunate person, just as you were helped.

—NAPOLEON HILL

13

VISUALIZATION

Man's greatness lies in his power of thought.

—BLAISE PASCAL

VISUALIZATION IS ONE of the most powerful processes available to us and one of the most useful in realizing the success that we desire in life. As Ella Wheeler Wilcox so aptly stated:

> *The thing thou cravest so waits in the distance,*
> *Wrapt in the silences, unseen and dumb,*
> *Essential to thy soul and thy existence—*
> *Live worthy of it—call, and it shall come.*

As executive director of the Napoleon Hill Foundation, I have my offices on the campus of the University of Virginia-Wise. One day a visitor asked me, "How do you put up with that building noise?"

I had taught myself not to hear the construction noises from next door, where a 116-student dormitory was being constructed.

In a sense, we can learn to see what we want to see, but the important point of being able to see what we want to see is what we do once we envision a better way. A Japanese proverb states it intelligently: "Vision without action is a daydream. Action without vision is a nightmare."

I have found that what someone receives as compensation is for his time and the duties that he is performing at present, but the biggest wages are paid to those who have the vision to see into the future.

I spent 38 years in the banking industry and 18 of those years in the top position at a savings and loan. I was hired at the age of 41—and not because of family connections or my own personal wealth, but probably because the bank was literally broke.

This was in 1983, when interest rates had soared out of sight (banks were paying around 20 percent for deposits) and 30-year fixed-rate mortgage loans on the books were paying from 6 percent up, but averaging less than 10 percent. This was a terrible situation, causing hundreds of banks to close. Savings banks were particularly hard hit for several reasons, but mainly because of a law that deregulated what rates could be paid for deposits.

Savings banks could not make consumer loans or commercial loans, which have shorter maturities and thus give the lender a chance to increase the rates it charges for loans. Home mortgages had fixed rates for up to 30 years. I relate this personal story not so much to impress you as to explain how I saw the situation and the vision I had for the future.

The bank had lost $1.5 million in the three previous years and had only $35,000 in capital left. Just before I came in as CEO, the examiners were planning to close the bank. I saw the future, which included rates coming down and the oil crisis actually helping the bank because the local area was a major producer of coal.

I went about my work with the thought that everything I envisioned would come true in the near future. At age 41, I signed a 10-year employment contract at a salary that was not huge, but would allow my family to live comfortably. What I saw in the contract was stock options for 200,000 shares at $3.00 per share. Even though the stock was worthless at the time, I saw myself as a millionaire.

To make this happen, I had to get the stock to $8.00. If I did so, with a cost of $3.00, I would have a million-dollar profit. I did not go about spending that future million dollars, but I saw myself there. Eventually I sold the stock for $14 or more per share.

I visited Sobel's, a famous men's store in nearby Kingsport, Tennessee. Sobel's was noted for having the best men's suits, and I remember my first trip there. The store had expert help, and it could measure you for a fine suit. A sign behind the cash register read, "If you are to be a success, first dress the part." I always remembered that sign, and I always dressed the part because the public expects it and tends to respect those who do.

While I was president of the bank, I was asked to teach an evening course that I originated at the University of Virginia-Wise. The course was always well attended. I remember one particular class that included a lawyer, a CPA, a doctor, and a multimillionaire businessman. I taught the course both semesters for several years until the governor of Virginia appointed me to the university's board. The university's bylaws do not allow professors to be on the board, so I no longer teach the course—although I do give guest lectures on occasion.

In one particular class, I had a student remark that it was not fair for people to be treated differently because they were dressed better or worse than others. I told the student that in life, one has to deal not only with what one perceives as fair, but with reality.

Recently I took my 89-year-old mother out of town to pay her respects to a distant relative. While we were at the reception, I was approached by one of the students from the first class I had taught at the University of Virginia-Wise. Julia McAfee was that student, and she reminded me that I had asked each student in my Keys to Success class to write down her goals. Julia told me that she had seen herself as a lawyer and that she still had her papers (remember that goals must be in writing so that they become a contract with yourself). Today she is a very successful lawyer and an outstanding person in the community.

I could relate many other success stories from students who were in the Keys to Success class. All of the students, I am sure, would agree that the material helped them in their lives. I know that, as the teacher, I learned a great deal, because preparing properly required effort on my part prior to each class.

It is important that you see yourself as a success, even though, by some people's standards, you may not be successful at the present moment.

Because I was able to see the future, the bank made $90,000 in the first full year of operation after I joined it, more than $200,000 in the second year, and so forth until 18 years had passed and it had been profitable every single year. Based on the profits, I received a new car, an increased salary, and other perks. I cashed out the last of my options at about the age of 60 and moved on to a new role with the Napoleon Hill Foundation.

But this is not a book about banking—or just about me—and I recount my experience in that industry only as an example of someone visioning the future and acting *as if* it were true until the vision becomes a reality. At the same time, I fully understand Ben Sweetland's statement that "success is a journey, not a destination."

To approach a problem that needs to be solved, you should first obtain worthwhile information on the problem. Today more than at any previous time in history, we are living in an information age. Problems require you to study facts and data if you seriously desire to solve them.

The great writer Elbert Hubbard said, "The greatest mistake you can make in life is to be continually fearing you will make one."

To solve problems, you must first visualize a solution in your mind.

Everything that takes on a material shape is a mental process first. Creativity comes from the mind: the ability to conceive solutions and to foster ideas that you did not have before you employed your thought process. Think in pictures of things that you want to happen; when you do so, more often than not, the future you envision can become a reality.

The use of your vision helps you to focus not on things as they are, but on things as you want them to be. For example, if you are overweight, the vision of your ideal weight can move you from the thought to the action to the reality of achieving that goal.

VISUALIZATION

Christian Kent Nelson, a Danish immigrant, owned a candy store to supplement his income as a schoolteacher.

In 1920, when a boy in his store in Iowa could not decide whether to spend his money on a chocolate bar or ice cream, Nelson came up with the idea of melting chocolate onto bars of ice cream. The new creation was originally sold under the name I-Scream Bars; later the name was changed to Eskimo Pie.

Nelson became independently wealthy as a result of a simple idea that he was able to visualize. You can do the same.

Remember, visualization is being able to see with your "inner eyes" what can become reality.

The use of visualization is very important in that you need to see or visualize what you want, not what you do *not* want. It is important that you focus on positive visualization. If you are poor, you want to see or visualize not poverty, but wealth. You must control your thoughts if you want to control your conditions. Events are likely to follow your thought process and become real, whether you desire them or not. Always remember the quote from Job: "For the thing which I greatly feared is come upon me." That is a perfect example of negative visualization.

In 1934, at the graduation at Wise High School in southwestern Virginia, the commencement speaker was Napoleon Hill, who wrote the eight-volume *Law of Success*. Hill had become so successful during the years of the Great Depression that the royalties from his book sales allowed him to purchase a Rolls-Royce, which attested to the tremendous demand for his writings on the philosophy of success.

Among the young graduates listening to Hill was Marvin Gilliam. This graduate from Wise High School attended Milligan College in Tennessee. After entering the U.S. Army, Gilliam served as a major with General George Patton in World War II. When the war was over, he returned to Wise High School, where he taught English and history.

I was a student of Mr. Gilliam's in high school, and I grew to appreciate the quiet genius that he was. I remember one particular day when he read from the poem "Andrea del Sarto" by Robert Browning, in which Browning writes, "A man's reach should exceed his grasp,/ Or what's a heaven for?" I have recalled this incident hundreds and hundreds of times throughout my lifetime. Mr. Gilliam's single explanation was that one should always try to improve oneself on a daily basis—simple yet profound advice.

After retirement, Mr. Gilliam and his wife, Betty, who taught art at Clinch Valley College, where I was later a student, moved to a nearby town.

One weekend, my wife and I were in the local shopping center, and as we were leaving a cafeteria after lunch, we met Mr. and

Mrs. Gilliam and had a very interesting conversation with them. Mr. Gilliam told me that he had read in the newspaper of my involvement with the Napoleon Hill Foundation, and during the conversation, he told me about his 1934 graduation with Napoleon Hill as the commencement speaker.

I asked Mr. Gilliam if he recalled what Hill had spoken about, and he said that Hill had talked about the power of thought. He further remembered that the Wise High School principal, L. F. Addington, had remarked on what an eloquent speaker Hill was. I could not wait to make notes on what my teacher had to say, based upon his own personal experience and eyewitness. I will always treasure my conversation with Mr. and Mrs. Gilliam on that day.

A few years later, I received a call from Mrs. Gilliam, telling me of Mr. Gilliam's death. She asked me to be a pallbearer, which I considered to be an honor.

In his classic *Think and Grow Rich!*, first published in 1937, Hill said, "There are no limitations to the mind except those we acknowledge. Both poverty and riches are the offspring of thought."

In March 2004, at the annual meeting of the board of trustees of the Napoleon Hill Foundation, I mentioned to the trustees that I would like to do a book on success among Hispanic Americans. I knew that the demographics in the United States were changing and that the Latino population was increasing at a rapid rate. Latinos were fast becoming an ever more important part of the labor market, and I thought the Napoleon Hill Foundation, with its background in self-help books, courses, seminars, and prison work, should recognize the Latinos and publish a book on successful Latinos and how they became successful. The book would serve as an inspiration to Latinos, showing that the United States was still indeed a land of opportunity, where anybody could become a success by following some simple principles. What better way could there be to share this message than through stories of and by successful Latinos who had become successes in various fields?

Phil Fuentes, a tremendously successful Latino and a trustee of the Napoleon Hill Foundation, remarked, "I know the person who would be ideal for the job." Phil was speaking of Lionel Sosa, a media expert and the creator of the largest Hispanic advertising agency in the United States.

Lionel became acquainted with the principles of success when he was working as a sign painter for $1.10 per hour. He was asked to create a sign advertising a class on the Napoleon Hill principles of success. His curiosity caused him to inquire as to what the classes were about, and after getting his answer, he borrowed the $200 needed to take the class. During the lesson on success, Lionel decided that rather than painting signs at $1.10 per hour to support his wife and children, he should form his own advertising agency.

Lionel started his own firm, known as Sosa and Associates, in 1980, and it became the largest Latino ad agency in the United States. You would be well advised to obtain Sosa's book, *The Americano Dream: How Latinos Can Achieve Success in Business and in Life*, and read the story for yourself.

In May 2004, Phil Fuentes arranged for me to travel to Chicago to attend the annual Latino banquet at the Hilton Chicago. I traveled with my daughter, Donna, who enjoyed meeting Lionel and his wife, Kathy. Kathy, like my daughter, is an interior decorator. I spent two days with Lionel and told him what I wanted to do. Lionel gave me a copy of his book and wrote inside, "To Don Green—My American Dream is to work for the Napoleon Hill Foundation and you!"

With the help of Robert Johnson, an attorney and a longtime assistant of the Napoleon Hill Foundation, we were able to structure an agreement under which Lionel would write stories of successful Latinos. Lionel got busy writing about Latinos like Alberto Gonzales, who became U.S. attorney general under President George W. Bush. Once the book was begun, we offered a major New York publisher the opportunity to review the first part of the manuscript, and the publisher indicated that it would like to publish the book first in hardcover, then in trade-paperback size, and finally in a pocket-sized paperback edition. Bob Johnson then prepared a contract with the publisher, and I signed on behalf of the Napoleon Hill Foundation.

The next step was marketing the book. Given the publisher's expertise and the media genius of Lionel Sosa, the idea of publishing a book for Latinos was looking good, to say the least. Lionel had an excellent background in marketing to the Latino population, especially in the United States.

Lionel had prepared advertisements for John Tower when he was running for the U.S. Senate from Texas. The campaign was successful, partially because of Latino support. Success breeds success, and Ronald Reagan sought Sosa's support in gaining the Texas and California Latino vote in both of his successful races for president. Later George W. Bush sought Sosa's help in his race for governor of Texas and in two successful presidential campaigns.

Finally, there were many meetings with the publisher and others, plus a meeting with CEO Lee Scott of Walmart to promote the book, titled *Think and Grow Rich: A Latino Choice*.

For those of you who are studying or reading this book because you were attracted by its title, remember, first there is a thought, which then develops into a vision. Then that vision has to be worked into a plan for action. The action will bring about a definite result.

Without action, a dream is just that; it may entertain you for a short period of time.

If need be, go back and read this section again and follow the simple steps that can turn an idea into a product that can produce millions of dollars in sales. Not only did the idea of a book give jobs directly in writing, editing, marketing, and sales, but it will no doubt have a profound positive effect upon the lives of its readers for this and future generations.

Our health is greatly influenced by eating right, exercise, proper sleep, and the like, but it is also affected by our mind, whether positively or negatively. Worrying is a form of negative imagination and can have a tremendous impact on our health. On the other hand, learning to create positive images can help eliminate stress and also change negative habits into positive habits.

Imagery is an important component of the processing of information and how we see things mentally. Images allow us to use thoughts to see, smell, or taste various things, or, in other words, use our senses to recapture our past from memories or envision our future through dreams and goals.

You control your destination, your wealth, and your happiness to the degree to which you can think about these elements of your future, visualize them, and see them to such a degree that you bring about their completion. Thus, the power that will enable you to lead a productive life is within your own mind.

The power of thought has often been compared to a fertile garden. With proper care, the fertile garden will be productive because of the attention it receives. If it is neglected, the garden will produce weeds. The mind is never at rest and is either building up or tearing down. It produces either riches or poverty, success or failure, misery or happiness. Nothing is more valuable to the human race than the mind, but only a tiny percentage of its capacity is used.

Depending on the way it is used, the power of thought is either the most beneficial or the most dangerous power that is available to man.

Great nations are built or destroyed through the power of thought.

All human creations are developed first in people's thoughts. It is the mind that first develops thoughts and then takes action that brings good or bad results.

The advantage people have over all other creatures is that each has the right to live her life as she wishes.

The power to choose is of profound importance because making the right choices will allow you to live a successful and happy life. Making the wrong choices or allowing others to make choices for you will most likely lead to an unsuccessful life.

Goals must be of your own making, just as you think your own thoughts. By choosing the correct goals and engaging in proper planning and actions, you can expect all your desires, whether they are wealth, health, fame, or peace of mind, to be fulfilled, which will help you acquire happiness.

If you don't have meaningful goals, you will need to set some if you are to reach your potential. Once you have set goals to guide your future, it is urgent that you have a belief system that tells you that you will accomplish your goals.

While I was working in the finance business, I was offered the job as second in command at a new bank. Once I had the job, I believed that I could become the chief executive officer of a bank. Not only did I compare myself to others in the position of CEO, but I believed that I needed only experience and the opportunity. It was important that I saw myself as a bank CEO. I continued to prepare myself for the job.

I applied my talents with a positive attitude and obtained results in my position that drew attention to me. I asked to be allowed to attend the Virginia Bankers School of Bank Management at the University of Virginia, and permission was granted. I gained a valuable education, but once I had graduated from the school, I was still not content.

I once attended a seminar at the Federal Reserve Bank in Richmond, Virginia. Upon reading material from the Federal Reserve, I noticed that the officers of the Federal Reserve were graduates of the Stonier Graduate School of Banking at Rutgers University. Again I saw an opportunity to further my education and better prepare myself for a future opportunity.

I asked for permission to attend the Stonier Graduate School of Banking for three summer sessions, and I was again given the chance to study under some of the best instructors in banking and to work on banking projects with other bankers from many parts of the world.

Approximately three years after I graduated from Stonier, I was offered the CEO job, as I have explained previously. I do not relate this story to boast, because many others have accomplished much more than I did. I relate it to show you that goals are important, along with plans, belief, and a course of action designed to get you where you have had a vision of being.

At this point, I remind you that the accomplishment itself is not the most important part of the experience. I'll repeat the quote from Ben Sweetland because he says it very well and succinctly: "Success is a journey, not a destination." It is what we become while we are on the journey that is the most important thing.

14

THINKING

All that we are is the result of what we have thought.

—THE BUDDHA (563–483 B.C.)

All riches have their origins in the mind.

TRUE WEALTH CONSISTS of ideas, not money. Money is only the material medium that is exchanged for ideas. Paper money in itself—yen, euros, or another currency—is worth nothing; it is the ideas behind it that give it value.

The whole point is that you should not go outside to seek wealth. Wealth lies within you. Use your mind to *think* in a constructive manner.

Thinking does not mean idly wasting time. You need to think with a purpose in mind and an end in view: trying to solve a problem. In *The Master Mind*, Theron Q. Dumont says that thinking is forced upon us when we are deciding on a course to pursue, perhaps a life's work to take up. This is the kind of thinking that was forced upon us in our younger days when we had to find the solution to a problem in mathematics, or when we tackled psychology in college.

When I talk about thinking, I do not mean holding petty opinions on a particular subject. I mean thinking about significant questions that lie outside the bounds of your narrow personal welfare. This is the kind of thinking that is now so rare—and so badly needed!

To seek to discover new worlds or new methods, you must do more than merely ponder. You must think in a constructive manner. The greatest discoveries have arisen out of things that everybody had seen, but only one person truly *noticed*. The biggest fortunes have been made from the opportunities that many people had, but that only one person took hold of.

Do you realize that the reality of poverty exists because the *fear* of poverty is visualized and thus brought into being? The lesson that the many millions of people who are in poverty have not yet learned is the law of supply.

The law of supply is that you must think abundance, see abundance, feel abundance, and believe abundance. No thought of limitations should enter your mind. It is not possible to desire anything of which, as far as the mind is concerned, there is not an abundant supply. If you can visualize it in your mind, you can realize it in your life.

The seeds of both prosperity and success need to be nourished with intense desire. Keep in your mind's eye the picture of the thing you want. You must realize that you think in pictures. Believe in your mind's eye, forget your fears, and realize that your future will be the one you make for yourself. There is nothing that can deter you if you set your goal, forget difficulties, and always keep the goal in your mind's eye. It is no mere boast that our mental condition enables us to make our lives what we will. The only limitations are those that we set on ourselves.

There can be no limitations without a belief in limitations.

Nothing can stand in the way of a will that wants—an intelligence that knows. The great thing is to start. "Begin," says Ausonius. "To have begun is half the work. . . . Again begin this, and thou wilt have finished."

Always believe that limitations will not apply to you, and remember that the great fortunes have been founded on great faith. One man's faith was in oil, another's in land, another's in minerals. You must learn to express your desires mentally before you can claim them physically.

See the things that you want as already being yours. Know that they will come to you at need. Then let them come. Think of them as yours.

Remember that the more you have to offer to society, the more riches will flow to you. Our ability to receive what we desire is located within us, and the only limits are in our capacity to receive it. For example, suppose you need to make a bridge across a stream in order to farm a piece of land. There are certain principles involved in any problem that needs to be solved. These principles are available to solve any problem, but you have to apply them.

You must understand these principles if you are to use them, and it is extremely important that you apply them to the task to which you are seeking a solution.

If you want to solve a problem involving wealth, for example, you must understand the problem and apply the principles needed for a solution.

The power of the mind makes it possible for you to use your abilities and set them to work for you.

You must first make a mental image of what you want to accomplish. You control your destination, your wealth, and your happiness to the extent to which you can think them, visualize them, and see them to such a degree that they come to pass.

All personal achievement starts in the individual's mind. Your personal achievement starts in your mind. The first step is to know exactly what your goal or problem is. To get a clear picture of your goal or problem, write it down and adjust it until you are sure that the words clearly explain what you desire.

Thomas Edison said, "Success is based on imagination plus ambition and the will to work."

The story of Archimedes is a great example from history about how the mind can work for each of us.

Archimedes was a famous mathematician and inventor in ancient Greece. The king asked Archimedes' help in determining whether a new crown made by a goldsmith was of solid gold. The king wondered whether all the gold that had been delivered to the goldsmith had been used or whether the goldsmith had kept some of it. He therefore asked Archimedes to determine the crown's purity, but without damaging it in any way.

Archimedes thought about the problem of determining the crown's purity for several days without a solution. Then one day he got into a filled bathtub, and the water spilled over the side. This gave him the answer in his mind, and he shouted, "Eureka!"

The answer that came to Archimedes was to take three vessels of the same dimensions, each containing an equal amount of water. He would then put the crown into the first vessel, the amount of gold the king had furnished the goldsmith into the second vessel, and an equal volume of silver into the third vessel, then calculate the difference in the amount of water that overflowed from each vessel.

Once he got this idea, Archimedes took action and put it to the test. His experiment proved that the goldsmith was a cheat, as the king had suspected. The goldsmith had used silver as an ingredient in an alloy and kept the gold that he replaced. The answer that Archimedes proposed is today a well-known principle. A body that is immersed in a fluid displaces as much weight as the weight of an equal volume of that same fluid.

Very few people recognize the possibilities created by the power of their thoughts. A lot of people simply accept their position in life and never visualize any station in life better than the one into which they were born. Perhaps you have heard this remark: when a person begins to accomplish bigger and better things, her friends and relatives will say, "She is trying to get above her raising."

You are not bound by the conditions of your birth. You can use your thoughts to remake your world. You can make your thoughts become reality. You can make your world different by changing your thoughts.

It is ideas that are responsible for all our progress. Human nature is such that we are never satisfied until each of us has the power within himself to become what he desires.

It is important that you control your thoughts and "see" only those images that you desire. You should keep your mind on the things that you want and away from the things that you do not want.

You will not improve if you concentrate on your past failures. It was Pascal who stated, "Our achievements of today are but the sum total of our thoughts of yesterday."

To be successful, you need to realize that you have the power within you to do so, then know what you want, focus your thoughts upon what you have a burning desire to obtain, and carry out your program with a singleness of purpose.

The classic book by James Allen, *As A Man Thinketh*, puts it this way: "Act is the blossom of thought, and joy and suffering are its fruits; thus does a man garner in the sweet and bitter fruitage of his own husbandry."

> *Our remedies oft in ourselves do lie, which we*
> *ascribe to heaven.*
>
> — SHAKESPEARE

Your mental image is what counts, whether it be good or bad. It was Collier's paraphrase of Thackeray who said, "The world is a looking glass and gives back to every man the reflection of his own thought." The world that we enjoy or have a distaste for is a reflection of the world within. Within our subconscious minds, we have thoughts of success or failure, poverty or wealth, and our conscious mind finds ways of bringing them into being.

Our thoughts can become realities, and it is important for us to remember that each of us is in control of her own thoughts. Thoughts are wholly within the control of the mind.

Poet Walt Whitman expressed the power of thought very clearly and simply when he said, "Nothing external to me can have any power over me."

We cannot change our past experience, but we can determine what our future experiences will be like. We can make the coming day just what we want it to be.

We can be today what we think today. Our thoughts are causes, and the conditions are the effects.

In most cases, the reason that people fail in life is that they first thought about failure. It is apparent that failure makes excuses, and worries undermine any confidence that these people may have.

We are not just the results of fate; we are our own fate. As Proverbs says, "As a man thinketh in his heart, so is he."

We are simply our past thoughts and the sum total of the things that these thoughts have attracted to us.

Successful people have little time to think of failure, while people who are failures let their time be filled with ideas of failure. Shakespeare left us a lot to think about when he said, "There is nothing either good or bad, but thinking makes it so." Understanding Shakespeare's words will enable you to control every law of nature.

Each of us makes his own world—and he makes it through his mind. It is a fact of life that no two people see the same thing in the same way. Thoughts are the causes. Existing conditions are merely effects. Each of us molds himself and his surroundings by directing his thoughts toward his desired goals.

One of the main differences between humans and animals is that animals' lives are controlled by temperature, climate, and seasons. Humans alone have been able to free themselves from natural forces to a great degree because they understand the relation of cause and effect.

The last frontier will have been passed when people have complete understanding of the mind.

People do not yet understand that we can achieve mastery over our own thoughts and feelings. That a person should fall prey to any thought that takes possession of her mind is assumed to be unavoidable. We think about an impending doom, and it takes control of our imagination and literally destroys us. If we get a splinter in a finger, we take measures to remove it; once we understand how to do so, it is just as easy to expel undesirable thoughts from the mind.

When a person is able to expel mental torment from her thoughts, she will find herself totally free.

If you intend to become a success, there is nothing that is more important to you than visualizing the success that you seek in the future. As individuals, we think in pictures, and it is necessary for us to "see" with our inner eyes what we wish to obtain. Let me give you an example from my experience that occurred more than 30 years ago. You can substitute where you see yourself in the future, take the steps I took, and obtain your desired results.

In the 1970s, my wife and I were living in the first house that we had ever owned. We had borrowed $16,000 and built a three-bed-room brick ranch-style house. The house was close to my work and convenient to the university where I was attending night classes to obtain a degree with a major in accounting and a minor in business.

Shortly after I graduated from college, I was offered a job in my hometown that turned out to be a tremendous opportunity in a new bank.

Going to work at the new bank meant that my wife, my daughter, and I had to move. At the time, we did not wish to sell the only house we had ever owned.

When we moved back to our hometown, we were unable to find a suitable house that we could afford, as we still owned our original house. We leased the house to a professional couple; this provided us with some cash, but not enough to buy the house we really wanted. So we purchased a condominium, which was easy to finance and was available at once.

Knowing that we did not intend to live in a condo for very long, we began looking at house plans. One day, on the back of a mag-azine of house plans, was a paint company's ad showing a picture of a house. At the time, we did not know whether this was simply an ad or whether the plans for this house were available. I took the full-page ad and placed it on the bathroom door, where it remained until it became a reality. This reminds me that once you set your goal on something for which you have a passion or burning desire, even though all the steps you will need to take are unknown, you will start to notice things and people that will get you to your destination.

I contacted the paint company, and I was advised that the picture in the ad was of an actual house that was located outside of Richmond, Virginia.

The next thing that happened was that I was asked by the bank's CEO to attend a seminar at the Federal Reserve Bank in, of all places, Richmond, Virginia.

Phyl, my wife, went with me to the Federal Reserve Bank, and after the meeting, we went to see the house that was in the ad. We talked to the builder and made arrangements to purchase a set of the building plans.

The house in question was a two-story structure made of Canadian cedar with a roof of cedar shingles. It had two porches set back into the house, unlike a typical house of today, which is built and then the porch is added. The porch on the upper story could be reached from the master bedroom. The house had a huge chimney with fireplaces in the family room and in the master bedroom.

We had previously decided that we should build the house on a wooded piece of land that was close to my work. The only problem was that there was no suitable land available—or so it seemed.

One day I was waiting for one of the bank's directors—the one who was also the bank's largest stockholder and who had interviewed me for the job. I told Jim what I wanted, and he told me of such a lot next to the house he had just built for an executive of his coal company.

The next obstacle was to find a builder in whom I had confidence. I approached a noted builder, but he told me that he had retired. I had known his family a long time, and I reminded him of favors that I had done for his family. So he agreed to come out of retirement and build his last house for me.

Other obstacles were overcome in a similar way, such as building the huge chimney, foundation, and fireplaces with native stone.

After some 30 years, my wife and I have seen no reason to live anywhere else. The house, like everything else worthwhile, started with a picture in someone's mind, and the picture developed until it became a reality.

I recount this story not to boast about having an expensive or elaborate house, but to help you realize that "thoughts are things." Anything you want must always be a thought before it can become a thing. If you get nothing else from this story, remember that we all think in pictures.

You can take the same steps recited in this story and expect like results.

The imagination is literally the workshop wherein are fashioned all plans created by man. The impulse, the DESIRE, is given shape, form, and ACTION through the aid of the imaginative faculty of the mind.
It has been said that man can create anything which he can imagine.

—NAPOLEON HILL

The mind has the benefit and use of both forms of imagination. Most inventors use the form known as *synthetic imagination*. The use of synthetic imagination permits us to take plans, ideas, products, and projects; simply rearrange, alter, or add to them; and thus bring about new products. Most of Thomas Edison's inventions fall into this category.

Creative imagination is the process by which the imagination uses infinite intelligence and receives new ideas. Creative imagination is used by the great minds, whether they are businesspeople, musicians, or writers, to create new ideas.

Frank Maguire is an example of someone who was able to apply ideas to create millions of dollars in revenue. A well-known speaker, motivator, teacher, innovator, and storyteller, Frank could best be described as a marketing genius of our time. As a young man, he served as vice president and head of programming for ABC Radio Networks, served as a communications consultant to Presidents John F. Kennedy and Lyndon B. Johnson, and was right-hand man to Colonel Harland Sanders, the founder of Kentucky Fried Chicken.

Frank was also one of the five original task force members who created the Special Olympics and Project Headstart.

Frank gave the readers of *Three Feet from Gold* excellent advice, and at the fabulously successful book launch, he told me the following story that best illustrates using one's imagination to create an idea. He then developed the idea, working together with experts to develop it and create businesses that made the owners rich and gave excellent jobs to hundreds of thousands of people.

When he was working as an assistant to Colonel Sanders of KFC, Frank said he got a call one day from Fred Smith, asking him to come to Memphis to discuss an idea that Fred had. Frank explained that the meeting took place at a Holiday Inn, and Fred took a napkin and drew a dot in the center of the napkin with lines running out from the center like the spokes of a wheel.

Fred said, "Frank, I am going to pick up small packages all over the United States, bring them to Memphis, and ship them out before dawn."

Frank replied, "Fred, that is the dumbest idea I have ever heard."

Fred said, "No dumber than selling fried chicken in a cardboard box."

This comment was in reference to the years Frank Maguire had spent marketing Kentucky Fried Chicken. Fred Smith was a 30-year-old who had originated his idea while he was in college. His professor had not been overwhelmed with Fred's term paper on his idea, but Fred Smith won Frank over, and Frank Maguire was one of the original members of the Federal Express Corporation.

Be careful with whom you share the ideas that come to you when you exercise your imagination. You are likely to hear from well-meaning friends such remarks as, "You are crazy," "You will lose your shirt," or "Nobody has ever done that successfully before."

Share your ideas with other people of vision who can assist you on your journey to success.

15

YOUR PERSONAL
SUCCESS EQUATION

The difference between a successful person and
others is not a lack of strength, not a lack of
knowledge, but rather a lack of will.

— VINCE LOMBARDI (1913–1970)

I HAVE LEARNED that so-called hunches or ideas are similar to intentions. Ideas and intentions are worthless unless they are acted on
and brought to fruition. Let me give you a recent example:

As noted before, I spent 38 years in finance and banking, 36 of
which were in management—including nearly two decades as CEO.
The bank had been on the list to be closed because it had lost all its
capital and was insolvent until I was hired. Newspaper and magazine
articles were written about its performance; one magazine called the

bank "a diamond in the rough." This is another story that has been told elsewhere, but it is only natural that the banking business is still in me.

More than three years ago, as of this writing, I saw that the real estate market was getting into trouble.

I picked up the phone and called James Oleson, a stockbroker with A. G. Edwards (now a part of Wells Fargo), and told him to sell every share of stock I owned. Jim asked, "What's going on? Don't you know that with all the profits you have, you will owe a lot of taxes?" I said, "Jim, I know that, but the stocks have been very profitable and capital gains taxes are only 15 percent, which I will be happy to pay because I think the whole economy is going to be in trouble with the mortgage industry in trouble."

When I saw the economy going downhill, I got the idea of doing a book on persistence. Recalling one of W. Clement Stone's personal books in my library, *Cycles* by Edward Dewey, my thinking came together. This book, which Mr. Stone had read, studied, and made numerous annotations in, told me that the economy does not always move in one direction. With the financial future threatened, it was a time to be persistent and not be defeated. I had the idea of teaching the timely need of persistence.

In *Think and Grow Rich!*, Hill told the story of R. U. Darby, a gold prospector who quit three feet from a rich vein of gold. I wanted to interview people and ask them why they did not quit when they were faced with obstacles. Knowing that this was a formidable job, and as I was the executive director of the Napoleon Hill Foundation, I obtained the assistance of authors Greg S. Reid and Sharon L. Lechter, and the result was *Three Feet from Gold*, published by Sterling Publishing (owned by Barnes & Noble).

The book became a bestseller on Amazon, Barnes & Noble Online, and the *Wall Street Journal* within three weeks of going on sale. The book, which is being licensed all over the world, started with a simple idea that was acted on.

When you, the reader, have an idea, just remember that you do not have to have all the answers. If you have a purpose so strong that it is a burning desire to accomplish your goal, then you need to get started. Here is a list that you can use as a guide, all the time not forgetting that ideas have no value until they are acted upon:

+ Write down the goal you wish to accomplish.
+ Locate those who have the expertise you need.
+ Control your thoughts and maintain a positive mental attitude (PMA).
+ Set a time for the goal to be accomplished.
+ Define your personal success equation.

$$(P + T) \times A \times A + F = \text{your success equation}$$

You need to combine passion (*P*), something that you get so excited about that you eat, sleep, and get up with it, and talent (*T*), something that you are good at. Next, multiply that sum by A, the right associations, which are those who have success as part of their being. You want expert aid, not the opinions of friends or relatives who would only burden you and harm your attempts. Action simply means steps in the right direction. You might say that with all of these ingredients, *just do it*. Add your faith (F), which is simply your belief in yourself. Without faith, you will be like most other people and simply quit when you encounter any obstacles. Now your success equation is complete.

16

PERSEVERANCE AND PASSION

We may affirm absolutely that nothing great in
the world has been accomplished without passion.

— HEGEL

THE REASON THAT definiteness of purpose is the starting point for all achievement is that when you have a strong enough reason to accomplish your goal, you will persevere and not give up when that going gets tough. Surely you have heard the old adage, "When the going gets tough, the tough get going." Holding on to a strong purpose all the way to a successful outcome means having determination to the very end.

During the Civil War, President Abraham Lincoln was asked, "How does Grant impress you as a leading general?" He replied,

"The greatest thing about him is cool persistency of purpose. He is not easily excited, and he has got the grip of a bulldog. When he once gets his teeth in, nothing can shake him off."

I would say that that is perseverance—putting your teeth of purpose into the goal you are seeking, and holding on until the object you desire is in your possession.

The offspring of persistency of purpose is the success that you and I seek.

Once a person is absolutely sure that he is on the right path, perseverance will be a tremendous benefit. President Calvin Coolidge had this to say about persistence: "Press on. Nothing in the world can take the place of persistence. Talent will not; nothing is more common than unsuccessful men with talent. . . . Education alone will not; the world is full of educated derelicts. Persistence and determination alone are omnipotent."

Don't desire anything in life unless you are willing to pay the price.

You can read self-help books by the ton, attend seminars, listen to audio messages, and get helpful information from most of these sources. But if you are to become a successful person, you cannot do better than to follow your dream, or, as I prefer to say, chase your desire with a passion. Napoleon Hill learned and wrote that the first step in personal achievement was to have a "burning desire."

This first step has always been the same, and it has not changed.

You are likely to suffer defeat or quit too soon if you lack this burning desire or passion to pursue your dream. Be certain that what you are doing is exactly what you desire and that you are not chasing money or what someone else desires. If you pursue something that you have a passion for, then the money will be secondary in your life. As John A. Shedd put it more than a century ago: "A ship in harbor is safe—but that is not what ships are built for."

Likewise, the Russian poet Boris Pasternak said, "It is not revolutions and upheavals that clear the road to new and better days, but . . . someone's soul, inspired and ablaze." It is ancient wisdom to "know thyself," to look inside one's soul for the answers.

> *What the superior man seeks is in himself; what the small man seeks is in others.*
>
> — CONFUCIUS

Concentrate your energies on making a success of one thing at a time. If you have too many irons in the fire at one time, you can find yourself unable to perform at your best. Be a specialist and learn to do one thing just a little better than others, and you will get your reward.

Never put off until tomorrow what you need to and can do today.

Success is measured by the ability to push forward a little each day. Learn to divide each day into proper proportions: get enough sleep, do enough work, get enough rest, and make enough happiness, and you will have a harmonious day.

Let's take a look at the concept of passion.

PASSION

Passion is a powerful emotion expressing strong beliefs or enthusiasm.

Walter Chrysler, the founder of Chrysler Corporation, took the wages he had saved and bought a new car. Instead of driving it, he took the car apart in order to improve it. This is passion, and it's no wonder that Chrysler was able to quote Ralph Waldo Emerson in saying, "Nothing great was ever achieved without enthusiasm."

Once you find your passion, you will love doing what you need to do to achieve it, while many others without passion will not be successful because they either do not apply their talents or quit. Without passion, you will lack the direction and focus that are necessary if you are to succeed.

Robert T. Johnson, Jr., developed a passion for reading at a very early age. In the first grade, Bob read 52 books, which was more than twice the number read by any other student. Bob's prize was a copy of the famous children's book *The Little Engine That Could.*

Bob later went to college at the University of Michigan, where he had the highest GPA in the freshman class. He was a very successful copyright lawyer for a prestigious firm in Chicago for 32 years. Passion does matter if you want success.

Find your passion and you will never "work" again.

"It need be no discouragement that you be obliged to hew your own way and pay your own charges. . . . I know this, for I did so when teachers' wages were much lower than they are now. It is a great truth, that 'where there is a will, there is a way.'"

The previous paragraph was written by James A. Garfield when he was a teacher of ancient languages at Hiram College, Ohio, at age 26. The letter was addressed to his young friend of 19 years, Burke Hinsdale. Twenty-four years after he wrote this letter of advice, Garfield had become the twentieth president of the United States and Burke Hinsdale was president of Hiram College.

Recently I was having lunch with a well-educated businessman, and he mentioned his son, who he said was a near genius with a photographic memory, yet despite his intelligence, he was going nowhere on the road to success. I reminded my friend that I no doubt had read more than a thousand books and that while my findings had led me to believe that intelligence was a good thing to have, it was no guarantee of success. In spite of his intelligence, if someone lacks a purpose, a will, a burning desire, passion, or whatever term you wish to apply, that person will not plan, make the right choices, and act to accomplish worthwhile deeds.

All activity and preparation are of little use without a purpose.

A person who has no purpose is comparable to a ship without a rudder, chart, or compass, tossed about on the sea. You could say that most people are trying to cross the ocean of life without a definite aim.

People without a purpose are headed more for a shipwreck than for a safe harbor.

Singleness of purpose means making a decision to follow a specified course, profession, or work in one's life. The purpose becomes an object that you must keep in view and continue striving toward not only when the going is easy, but also when the course is difficult. That is what the Apostle Paul was referring to when he said, "This one thing I do." This purpose became Paul's life work, meaning that all his energy was directed toward that accomplishment, and when he said, "I press toward the mark for the prize," he simply meant that this was his purpose in life and that he had a will and determination that would not accept defeat.

Perhaps the wise man said it best, when his advice was, "Let thine eyes look right on, and let thy eyelids look straight before thee. Ponder the path of thy feet, and let all thy ways be established. Turn not to the right hand nor to the left." You could not find better advice with regard to the importance of singleness of purpose.

> *If you create an act, you create a habit. If you*
> *create a habit, you create a character. If you create*
> *a character, you create a destiny.*
>
> —ANDRÉ MAUROIS

You have the power to choose. First Lady Eleanor Roosevelt noted: "In the long run, we shape our lives, and we shape ourselves. The process never ends until we die. And the choices we make are ultimately our own responsibility."

There is a wonderful little book about our right to choose our future, *Your Greatest Power*, by J. Martin Kohe, that requires about 30 minutes to read.

You own a wonderful asset, and if you use it correctly, it will help give you confidence and peace of mind. The use of this powerful asset will permit you to move in the direction of your chief aim or purpose in life. The right application of this asset will turn failure into success.

If you experience a number of failures, it may seem that failure is your lot in life, no matter what you try. After a string of failures, you could easily come to believe that life is just difficult, that you have been dealt a bad hand of cards, and that the deck of life is stacked against you, so why even try any more, as you can't win. You can even convince yourself that no matter what you do, the results are not going to be what you desire.

If you have fallen into this trap, you need to discover this great power that will change your life. To change your direction in life, you must recognize this greatest power and use it to change your circumstances for the better.

While I was a bank president, one of the major employers in the area was a large coal company. When this company closed its coal mine, it put several hundred employees out of work. These employees were accustomed to making very good wages—more than $40,000 a year, on average, plus very liberal benefits. Many of these coal miners were customers of the bank, and in several instances, I heard them tell what happened. Some blamed the company; many signed up for disability. Some no doubt had injuries, because underground coal mining is a hazardous job. I have personal experience because my father was a coal miner and was seriously injured more than once.

The right to choose, your greatest power, was never more apparent than in these people's reactions to being unemployed. Some of the coal miners took their unemployment as a time to pause and reflect upon their lives. Many of them continued their education at the local colleges, and others were able to obtain jobs that in some instances were better than the jobs that they had lost.

Often a person who has lost her job or had other difficulties to contend with will adopt the attitude that life is difficult, life is unfair, the employer was crooked, the cards are stacked against her . . . so what is the use? You can't win. Such a person puts forth little or no effort and is firmly convinced that no effort is worthwhile because no matter what she does, she will not succeed. Once people have lost their desire to win in life, they simply accept their fate and probably use what energy they have to blame others.

These people will make statements such as, "Rich people are crooks," "They inherited their wealth," "The government has too many taxes," "Prices are too high," or any other excuse, pointing fingers everywhere but failing to look in the mirror.

Whenever people are experiencing failure, they are simply failing to discover this great power that will surely change their lives. They don't recognize it. They don't even know it exists. They can see others struggling just as they are, and their thoughts about their condition are that this is life.

Raimundo de Ovies tells a tale about the time the great library at Alexandria, Egypt, burned, and only a single book was saved. A poor man bought the book for a few coppers. The book was not very interesting, but it contained a strip of vellum on which was written the secret of the "Touchstone."

The touchstone was a small pebble that could turn common metal into pure gold. The written message was that the touchstone could be found on the shores of the Black Sea, among all the other pebbles that looked like it. But the secret to the touchstone was that the real stone would feel warm when it was touched, while the other ordinary stones would feel cold.

The poor man who had bought the book with the message sold what few possessions he had and went to the seashore. He had a plan to become rich by finding the pebble that was warm to the touch.

The man knew that he could not just pick up a pebble that felt cold and throw it down; if he did, he could be picking up the same pebble hundreds of times. His plan was that once he had picked up a pebble and found it to be cold, he would simply throw it into the sea. This plan allowed him to pick up a pebble only once.

The man spent a whole day picking up pebbles, but none of them was the touchstone. Then he spent a week, a month, a year, three years, but he did not find the touchstone. However, he was determined, and he continued to pick up a pebble, discover it was cold, and throw it into the sea.

He continued this same routine day after day.

Finally, on a beautiful morning, he picked up a pebble, and it was warm. However, he threw it into the sea. Simply put, he had formed such a habit of throwing the pebbles into the sea that when he found the warm pebble that he desired … he threw it away.

The story of the touchstone is like us. How often have we had this great power, the power to choose, and failed to recognize it? No doubt we have had this great power in our hands and then thrown it away because we failed to recognize it.

The power to choose is the greatest power that a person can possess.

Napoleon Hill published his all-time bestselling book *Think and Grow Rich!* in 1937. This book has probably influenced more people than any other so-called self-help book ever written. It has certainly influenced me. The title itself had a tremendous effect on the book's success. Hill chose *Think and Grow Rich!* as the title after he had completed the manuscript and sent it to the publisher. No other title could have had the same positive results as *Think and Grow Rich!* The title tends to jump out at you, and how could anyone who was looking for success not be attracted to it? I think the answer to the attraction that the title *Think and Grow Rich!* has to a potential buyer of books on self-help, motivation, or a desire to become wealthy is obvious.

The book was such a success that even though it was published at the height of the Great Depression, was priced at a then hefty price of $2.50, and lacked the type of advertising that is available today, it sold out in a matter of weeks. It was printed again with a larger quantity and quickly sold out again. *Think and Grow Rich!* was printed a total of three times in 1937 and has been continuously in print ever since.

Most so-called bestsellers are available in retail bookstores for a period of two years or less, and if you want a particular book with a publication date several years back, you must do a book search to get a copy.

Napoleon Hill's choice has had overwhelming positive results, and its benefit is still being felt today, not only in the United States, but all over the world. *Think and Grow Rich!* is one of the most copied titles of all time.

Many authors continue to publish books, some of them worthwhile and others of very poor quality, with variations on the title by changing one word, thus trying to use the popularity of *Think and Grow Rich!* to promote their own books. Again, the power to choose, as exercised by Dr. Hill in his choice of title, has been proven through the book's continued popularity all over the world 75 years later.

As executive director of the foundation named in Hill's honor, I recently spent several weeks in Japan, China, Singapore, Hong Kong, and Malaysia, and I visited bookstores in each country. I observed firsthand the popularity of Napoleon Hill's books, many of which were published legally and many of which were pirated copies on which no royalty was being paid. The popularity of the books in foreign countries is further evidence of the effect of Napoleon Hill's making use of this greatest power . . . the power to choose.

How often has each person been confronted with this great power and failed to recognize it?

The effects of making a choice to give up remind me of the words of William Moulton Marston when he said, "On the plains of hesitation, bleach the bones of countless millions who, on the threshold of victory, sat down to wait, and in waiting, died."

17

LEGACY

Lives of great men all remind us
We can make our lives sublime,
And departing, leave behind us
Footprints on the sands of time;
Footprints, that perhaps another,
Sailing o'er life's solemn main,
A forlorn and shipwrecked brother,
Seeing, shall take heart again.
Let us, then, be up and doing,
With a heart for any fate;
Still achieving, still pursuing,
Learn to labor and to wait.

— HENRY WADSWORTH LONGFELLOW

THE MOTTO OF the Napoleon Hill Foundation is, "Making the world a better place in which to live." If you believe that life has

194 ❖ EVERYTHING I KNOW ABOUT SUCCESS I LEARNED FROM NAPOLEON HILL

purpose or meaning, then you can leave a legacy that helps make the world a better place.

The decisions that you make—or do not make—will help determine the type of legacy you leave behind. Whether you are part of the solutions to the cries for help or part of the problems that confront the human race will be a result of your actions on a daily basis.

If you go to the *Webster's New World Dictionary* and look for the word *legacy*, one of the meanings is: "anything which has come to one from an ancestor, predecessor, etc."

> *No person was every honored for what he received.*
> *Honor has been the reward for what he gave.*
> — CALVIN COOLIDGE

Millions of people have read *The Richest Man in Babylon* by George S. Clason since it was first written in 1926. The fable is interesting, and many people, like me, got the message and applied the suggestions to reach a life of financial security. Referred to as "Babylonian parables," *The Richest Man in Babylon* is an inspiring group of stories that teach thrift, finance, how to acquire money, and how to save part of the money you earn and use those savings to earn even more money.

The basis of *The Richest Man in Babylon* is that a part of all you earn is yours to keep. Here is where most people fail when it comes to wealth accumulation. People who fail not only do not keep part of what they earn, but by taking on debt for personal use make it more difficult to increase their wealth.

While the story of *The Richest Man in Babylon* gives wonderful advice, it is only a parable, that is, a simple story that teaches a lesson.

The story told in *The Richest Man in Babylon* is comparable to the story of Andrew Carnegie, except that the story of Carnegie's life is true. His biography is part of American history and much more fascinating than the "richest man" parable.

Andrew Carnegie was born in Scotland in 1835, and his family moved to the United States and settled in Pennsylvania. Carregie began working in a cotton factory at the age of 13. The youngster was greatly blessed by the existence of a local citizen who allowed young working boys like Carregie to use his library. Most of Carregie's education came through his love of books, and it provided him the means to secure positions of greater responsibility until he became superintendent of the Pennsylvania Railroad.

By 1865, Andrew Carnegie started the first of his many companies, building bridges, locomotives, and rails. When Carnegie sold it to J. P. Morgan in 1901, the Carnegie Steel Company was valued at $400 million and was the basis of the organization that became the U.S. Steel Corporation.

By 1870, Carnegie began to make his many philanthropic gifts. He is best known for his free public library buildings. In all, Carnegie made gifts to more than 2,500 communities. No doubt, his love of books and his memories of the great benefit he derived from reading led Carnegie to place such heavy emphasis on philanthropic gifts to libraries.

In 1889, Carnegie wrote *The Gospel of Wealth*, in which he stated his view that the rich are merely "trustees" of their wealth and have a moral obligation to distribute that wealth to promote the welfare and happiness of the common person. Carnegie was a prolific writer, but the quotation for which he is most famous is this: "The man who dies thus rich dies disgraced."

When Carnegie retired in 1901, his aim was to distribute his fortune. Not only did he make gifts to establish more than 2,500 libraries, but he provided organs to hundreds of churches. He was the benefactor to numerous colleges, schools, and nonprofit organizations in his native Scotland, the United States, and other parts of the world. Not only did Carnegie do all this, but he also set up several trusts and institutions bearing his name.

By the time Andrew Carnegie died in 1919, he had given away about $350 million during his lifetime, and his legacy continues today as a result of his gifts to those same trusts and institutions.

Most people will not leave a legacy that can compare with Andrew Carnegie's in terms of monetary contributions for the benefit of humanity. But almost everyone can leave a legacy in one form or another, and it need not be monetary in nature.

> *The highest reward for a person's toil is not what*
> *he gets for it, but what he becomes by it.*
>
> —JOHN RUSKIN

I have firsthand knowledge of many stories about leaving a legacy that I learned while I was in banking. I can think of no better way of leaving a legacy that will truly help make the world a better place in which to live than helping to educate our youth in this and future generations.

While I was working as a banker, two of my customers were an aunt and uncle of mine. Uncle Clint was my mother's brother, and he was one of 16 children. As he had only a third-grade education and his mother had died in her forties, it did not appear that Uncle Clint was destined for success or would leave a legacy for future generations.

Uncle Clint worked as a coal miner for most of his life. Though wages are high today, when he started, he worked for about $3 per day and was making about $20 per day when he retired.

He lived in a small town, and he built some rooms behind his house to rent to construction workers and salespeople; this enabled him to make some extra money. Clint and his wife, Lucille, were unable to have children, and by living very frugally, they saved the money they received less their living expenses.

Clint and Lucille visited my office once a month for years and years, seeking advice. They did not invest in anything but certificates of deposit. Lucille died about two years before Clint. Prior to his death, I had helped my aunt and uncle have their wills prepared by a local attorney, William J. Sturgill. Mr. Sturgill, a longtime supporter of the University of Virginia and a personal friend, prepared the wills for free.

Clint and Lucille had accumulated $1.2 million—basically all cash and with no debt.

I spent many a lunch hour with Clint and Lucille, helping them plan what to do with their wealth. The money was designated for such causes as $100,000 to the local cancer treatment center, a like amount to St. Jude's Children's Hospital, and the Shriners Crippled Children's Fund. The largest single gift was $500,000 to the University of Virginia as an endowment for scholarships.

Upon Clint's death at age 91, cousins Haskell Lambert, W. C. Lambert, and I became executors of his estate. After paying the will's bequests for such items as cemetery upkeep and a local children's park, the balance available to the university actually came to more than $700,000.

Today about 40 young people are receiving scholarships, and the endowment balance is now more than $800,000. Future generations will be better off as a result of the gifts the Lamberts provided. Even though they had very little formal education and never set foot on the college campus themselves, their legacy has been assured by their generosity.

It was Andrew Carnegie, the founder of U.S. Steel and one of the world's richest persons, who said, "Surplus wealth is a sacred trust which its possessor is bound to administer in his lifetime for the good of the community."

One spring, young Andrew Carnegie had some rabbits that multiplied very rapidly, and feeding them quickly became a problem. Little Andrew promised his playmates to name a rabbit for each boy who would pick cloves and dandelions to feed the rabbits. His first experience as an employer of labor was a huge success.

Andrew Carnegie was not interested in the technical details of his businesses and knew very little about mechanical processes. But he understood human needs, behaviors, and aspirations and had a system of incentives that attracted men to work for him.

In 1908, the young Napoleon Hill was sent to interview Andrew Carnegie. Can you imagine the scene? Hill was sent to Carnegie's 45-room mansion in New York City, overlooking Central Park. Hill had, of course, been born in a log cabin in the backwoods of southwestern Virginia.

Carnegie himself had started at the very bottom of the economic ladder, but he had reached the pinnacle of financial success when Hill, representing *Bob Taylor's Magazine*, interviewed him. Carnegie stressed definiteness of purpose and self-confidence as being his cardinal rule for personal achievement.

Carnegie introduced Hill to well-known, successful people, and over the next 20 years he interviewed more than 500 of them, including Thomas Edison, John D. Rockefeller, Henry Ford, George Eastman, and other giants of industry.

> *Never doubt that a small group of thoughtful,*
> *committed citizens can change the world. Indeed,*
> *it is the only thing that ever has.*
>
> — MARGARET MEAD

World-famous anthropologist Margaret Mead's statement is very true, and the same can be said of each of us. Our deeds and acts of kindness can extend beyond our lifetime in a positive manner, and that is what it means to leave a legacy.

C. Bascom Slemp, whose interest and influence was responsible for the creation of the Southwest Virginia Museum, is such a person. The Southwest Virginia Museum is a delight to visit. It is well maintained by Sharon Ewing, a good friend, on behalf of the Department of State Parks.

The museum is located in Big Stone Gap, Virginia, and had previously been the residence of General Rufus A. Ayers, the onetime attorney general of Virginia and a leader in the development of Wise County. Entering the Civil War at the age of 15, Ayers became a very successful lawyer, banker, and real estate mogul with interests in coal mining, lumber businesses, and politics.

Mr. Slemp was born in Lee County on September 4, 1870, and died on August 7, 1943. If he had done nothing other than found the museum, his legacy would have been assured. However, he was a member of the U.S. Congress from 1907 to 1922, and from 1923 to 1925, he served as secretary to President Calvin Coolidge.

While the museum today is famous for its collection of historical artifacts and the big stone mansion that houses the history of the pioneer way of life, it is the Slemp Foundation that best shows Mr. Slemp's generosity and his legacy.

A few years ago, I was invited to the museum when some of the area's most famous citizens were being honored. I was there to represent Dr. Napoleon Hill, the local author known all over the world. Among the other people recognized on the Walk of Fame were former governor Linwood Holton, authors Adriana Trigiani and Lee Smith, actor George C. Scott, and Dr. Andrew T. Still, founder of the American School of Osteopathy Medicine. Each of these individuals has created a powerful legacy, and some are still doing so today.

At his death, Mr. Slemp left about $350,000, which was invested by a bank, and the will designated that it be used to benefit the residents of Lee and Wise Counties. The trustees of the Slemp Foundation, such as Nancey Smith, the foundation's president, have been excellent stewards of the Slemp estate. More than $20 million has been given to Lee and Wise Counties, and this has greatly enhanced the ability of hundreds of young people to attend college as well as aiding in the construction of buildings on both high school and college campuses.

You do not have to leave an estate of millions or one that can grow to millions with good investments—many acts that are not monetary can create a legacy. The legacy we build is created by the decisions that we make on a daily basis.

Dr. Joe Smiddy, chancellor emeritus of the University of Virginia-Wise, is such a person. He has created a legacy without the use of millions of dollars. "Papa Joe," as he is affectionately known by his friends, helped thousands of young people get a higher education.

Many of the students that Papa Joe helped were of the first generation to attend college. Many of these students—like me—had parents who had not attended high school. When one or both of a student's parents attended college, it is very likely that that student will attend college. In a remote area, opportunity to attend college was not easy to come by.

Papa Joe grew up on a farm and was able to attend college because of the kindness of a school principal, who suggested Lincoln Memorial University in Harrogate, Tennessee. Having no money, Papa Joe, with an extra pair of work clothes, got a ride, made it to college, and worked on the college farm at 25¢ per hour to earn his way. When he became college chancellor and saw so many students in dire need of financial help, perhaps he was reminded of the care and attention he had been given. This was in the mid-1950s, and students did not have the resources that they have today.

Papa Joe would solicit contributions from businesspeople and friends and would even resort to taking funds collected from parking tickets to help a student in need. You can easily see why the students who became successful, whether as teachers, doctors, lawyers, bankers, or other professionals, were fortunate to have been influenced by Papa Joe.

**Choose your mentors carefully because if you learn
the principles of success and apply them some day,
you will probably surpass their accomplishments
and leave your own legacy.**

The greatest service a person can possibly give to humanity is encouragement to gain confidence in oneself, assurance of one's own power, and, more than anything else, the power to conquer the most potent and insidious enemy that has ever attacked the human race—*fear.* This is the message from the pen of Orison Swett Marden, who wrote of his experiences on the road to success.

Lee Iacocca, the legendary auto executive who was very successful at Ford Motor Company, then went to Chrysler as CEO and literally saved Chrysler from going out of business, will no doubt be remembered for his management skills. What we also need to recall when Lee Iacocca's name is mentioned is his remark quoting Elbert Hubbard, "No matter what you've done for yourself or for humanity, if you can't look back on having given love and attention to your own family, what have you really accomplished?"

What Iacocca's statement means is that success begins with one's family and that if one wishes to leave a legacy, then his family is the logical place to start.

Many people become well known for their accomplishments in their work, whether it be in sports, business, or entertainment. People such as Oprah Winfrey, Tom Cruise, and Donald Trump have become celebrities who are known the world over and hero-worshipped. But each will be remembered for the good that he or she has contributed to society. Wealth can be quickly lost. Maybe when Andrew Carnegie said, "He who dies rich dies disgraced," he was telling us that from those to whom much has been given, much is expected.

The following well-known personality is creating a legacy that is having positive effects on our most prized possessions—our youth. This is a person of whom I have firsthand knowledge.

Dolly Parton, born in the small town of Sevierville, Tennessee, at the edge of the Great Smoky Mountains National Park, has accomplished remarkable things and influenced the lives of thousands, if not millions, of people around the world with her talent and her philanthropy.

John Ruskin, the nineteenth-century English writer, wrote: "You will find that the mere resolve not to be useless, and the honest desire to help other people, will, in the quickest and most delicate ways, improve yourself."

I will admit that at the beginning of my career, it was money, money, money that motivated me, because I never thought I had enough. As I grew older, I learned what philosophers and other wise men had told us—that happiness would be found not in more possessions, but in providing a useful service to others. Dr. Albert Schweitzer encapsulated it well when he said, "The purpose of human life is to serve, and to show compassion and the will to help others."

As you travel on your personal journey to success, you will find out for yourself that happiness is found in service.

As Tom Brokaw once noted, "It is easy to make a buck. It's a lot tougher to make a difference."

As we are all a part of this earth, we should naturally have the desire to help others. The late Albert Schweitzer probably said it best: "You must give some time to your fellow men. Even if it's a little thing, do something for others—something for which you get no pay but the privilege of doing it."

> *All of our dreams can come true—if we have the*
> *courage to pursue them.*
>
> —WALT DISNEY

The author Orison Swett Marden wrote that we must have castles in the air before we can have castles on the ground. Napoleon Hill wrote that thoughts are things. Hill was simply expressing the same thing as Marden: everything begins in our thought process.

And so does it end there.

INDEX

ABOUT THE AUTHOR

DON M. GREEN is currently the executive director of the Napoleon Hill Foundation.

Graduating with a BA (Accounting and Business) degree at the East Tennessee State University, Don Green went on to study advanced phases of banking at the Stonier Graduate School of Banking at Rutgers. With banking as his natural flair, Don elevated himself from the bottom rung of the banking industry to become bank president and CEO—a position he served for nearly 20 years.

His meteoric rise in his career was matched by his diverse contributions to community and the commercial fraternity. His public offices spanned a spectrum that included educational institutions, hospitals, charitable causes, community service organizations, and arbitration boards. He was president of his county's Chamber of Commerce and president of the Foundation Board of the University of Virginia's College at Wise—a position in which he still proudly serves. Don is also a board member of the UVA/Wise Board of Trustees. His memberships include the Hoge Masonic Lodge, the Kiwanis Club, and the Shriners movement.

Don collected the Outstanding Citizen of the Year Award in 1996; the Sam Walton Business Leader Award in 1998; the William P. Canto Memorial Education Award in 1999; and the Volunteer of the Year Award (University of Virginia) in 2000.

Don organized and was successful in getting a 3-hour credit course, Keys to Success, included in the UVA/Wise curriculum based on the success principles of Napoleon Hill. Don taught the course for several years, and it is still a very popular course with students.

Under Don's leadership, many scholarships have been endowed as well as fully funding the Napoleon Hill professorship in the business department.

Thanks to Don and the Napoleon Hill Team, the popularity of Napoleon Hill's writings continues to have a positive effect on audiences all over the world.